TRAVERSING THE
Valley of Death

TRAVERSING THE
Valley of Death

A PRACTICAL GUIDE FOR
CORPORATE INNOVATION LEADERS

Stephen K. Markham
Paul C. Mugge

With a foreword by
Robert B. Tucker
Founder and President, The Innovation Resource, and
best-selling author of seven books on innovation

www.TraversingTheValleyOfDeath.com

Markham, Stephen, K.

Mugge, Paul, C.

Traversing the Valley of Death:
A practical guide for corporate innovation leaders

1. Innovation.   2. Industry.   3. Leaders.

Softcover
ISBN 978-0-9909853-1-0

Printed in the United States of America
Book Cover /Interior Design - Cyn Macgregor

INDUSTRY ENDORSEMENTS

For someone who was in a leadership position facing disruptive change in a biopharma business, I found myself in the position of being on both the "fuzzy" front end and accountable for the innovation implementation. The CIMS System for Industrial Innovation provided the framework for my leadership team to engage in hands-on work sessions generating outputs that created key work process milestones that became innovation building blocks. Yes, there were times during the journey where we felt stuck and confused, but the system provided us with the compelling rationale and a structured process to work through the obstacles and enabled us to regain focus and achieve our step-function objective. These skill sets are now institutionalized with the organization and have created confidence with my leadership team as we continue to navigate through the transformational change taking place in the health care industry.

—Lou Arp, President, Oncology Demand Chain Unit and General Manager,
Eisai Pharmaceuticals

Managing the development of new products is one of the most complex challenges facing organizations. Too often, even successful practices are not sustained over time, because too often they depend on the skills of key individuals rather than deeply installed practices. While our understanding of effective practices has deepened as a result of important research in the field, the translation of these insights to practice has not always followed. Markham and Mugge address this challenge by providing a detailed and disciplined path to sustainable success in creating new goods and services. Their book contains a series of focused templates and specific suggestions that lead directly to improved, sustainable practices that will improve any organization's effectiveness in extending and revitalizing their product portfolios.

—Thomas P. Hustad, Professor Emeritus of Marketing, Kelley School of
Business, Indiana University, and former President and longtime Board Member
of the Product Development & Management Association

As an innovation leader, I know the odds for mature companies to realize the benefits of breakthrough innovations are high; 1 in 10 would be outstanding! The wisdom and methodology in this book is a veritable survival guide to "traverse this Valley of Death" and come out the other side! Markham and Mugge are to innovation what Lewis and Clark were to North America–teaching us how to identify and use the local flora and fauna (Chapters 1-3), to translate the native's language (Chapters 4-5), and to draw the maps to guide us safely across the new territory (Chapter 6-7). Using the proven and systematic processes presented in this book, established companies can successfully and repeatedly generate top-line growth from disruptive innovations in products and services.

—Martha J. Collins, R&D Director, Air Products and Chemicals

For millennia, the standard response when approaching the Valley of Death has been prayer. Steve Markham and Paul Mugge aren't saying that's a bad idea, but they add greatly to the understanding of the situation, and go beyond academic knowledge to provide templates for building bridges and negotiating pitfalls. Steve began his academic pursuit of this understanding (with Center for Innovation Management Studies funding) 30 years ago while a graduate student at Purdue University studying the decisions and tactics used by "champions" to support technological innovation in industry. His career as an innovation researcher and practitioner/consultant is ongoing, and his knowledge of the Valley is deep and well-documented in this book. Paul's experiences at IBM as an internal "turn-around" warrior during the early 1990s honed his suspicion of easy fixes to the problems encountered in traversing the Valley. Paul continues to test his ability to find reliable paths through the Valley by working closely with CIMS' sponsoring firms as a coach and mentor to leaders of innovation. This is a book to keep close at hand.

—Al Bean, Founder and Executive Director Emeritus,Center for Innovation
Management Studies (CIMS)

Understanding the Valley of Death is an essential component to transforming innovation from a corporate aspiration to a practical driver of change. It underscores the fact—often unrecognized—that innovation, in particular the kind that is truly transformative, must be intentional so that good ideas become an impacting force that achieve business objectives in a consistent manner. This book provides essential insight for those business leaders that want to change innovation from a chance event to a predictable driver of corporate success and renewal. The handbook-feel is a refreshing approach to a topic that is frequently handled in an overly esoteric framework. This book will provide both established and aspiring innovators with an engaging approach to up their concept-to-fruition game.

—Juan Torres, SVP, Global Quality, Biogen Idec

When we started down the path of building a disruptive innovation capability, our initial benchmarking efforts revealed that a systemic approach to "Big" innovation was not at all commonplace. Through our engagement with NC State University's Center for Innovation Management Studies, we became aware of the System for Industrial Innovation and have begun embedding it in the fabric of our organization. The System represents a simple and comprehensive way of establishing operational rigor for an activity frequently seen as intangible and serendipitous. It has become key in our drive to establish a robust culture of innovation at Kelly.

—Rolf Kleiner, Chief Innovation Officer, Kelly Services

I have had the benefit of living through multiple instances of the old saw, "most innovations fail, companies that don't innovate die." The Valley of Death is littered with the bones of innumerable companies from young startups to venerable icons of American industry that missed this crucial point. A couple of decades ago, IBM came close to suffering that fate, and Paul Mugge was crucial in helping turn that company around based on market driven innovation. At Bell and Howell we are institutionalizing the innovation management culture espoused by Steve and Paul to drive our future.

—Ramesh Ratan, CEO, Bell and Howell

Almost three decades ago, the National Science Foundation Industry/University Cooperative Research Centers Program (I/UCRC) launched its first non-engineering I/UCRC, the Center for Innovation Management Studies (CIMS). Through the able leadership of Dr. Al Bean it become an unqualified success by showing how to bridge academic innovation studies with industry commercial practice. With the publication of *Traversing the Valley of Death*, Markham and Mugge have continued CIMS's pioneering tradition by utilizing its large data base to produce a book, complete with useful worksheets, that clearly and concretely explains how cutting-edge research can be translated into commercialized products, processes or services. I believe this is a guide that university researchers, entrepreneurs and innovation executives will find very informative.

—Alex Schwarzkopf, Contractor, National Science Foundation

The pace of innovation has been accelerating over the last decade, especially in the consumer electronics industry. Thus, the need for accelerating the pace of identifying and generating the front-end of innovation has dramatically increased. Furthermore, in the current highly competitive industrial environment, the execution and commercialization of innovative ideas to drive growth with a high probability of success with the ever-increasing degree of technological complexity is the key to success for all successful companies. The ecosystem and the systematic approach that is prescribed in *Traversing the Valley of Death* to execute industrial innovation enable the KEY to successful monetization of innovation.

—Sung Han, Technology Director, Eastman Chemical Co.

What an outstanding approach to managing innovation! This book is a must-read for senior level organizational leaders if only to survive this highly competitive global economy. The authors present a step-by-step guide to implement breakthrough innovation, covering the entire innovation life cycle: starting with innovation strategy planning and development—converting ideas into opportunities and creating the compelling business case, and completing the life cycle with adoption and implementation of the innovation product(s).

The use of Big Data for Discovery activities in the front-end of innovation and the tool kit provided offer valuable project and program management processes, tools and techniques to successfully traverse the

Valley of Death, hence fully implement breakthrough innovation. I highly endorse the breakthrough innovation approach presented in this book and encourage readers who haven't tried CIMS System for Industrial Innovation in their shops, to get it and start utilizing the System. We need to create the innovator mindset in our shops; and the authors' breakthrough innovation approach is the best tool to get us past the Valley of Death, and into implementation of innovative products.

—Victoria Kumar, PMP; Proprietor, Project Management Leaders Training and Project Management Institute Registered Education Provider

The innovation literature is replete with academic books written for other academics and seat-of-the-pants practice books written by and for other innovation and commercialization practitioners. In *Traversing the Valley of Death* Markham and Mugge have succeeded in bridging these two traditions by delivering a volume on innovation and commercialization that is informed by a scholarly understanding of the literature but delivers implementable guidance based on several decades of hands-on experience and close university and industry collaboration. While the authors know traversing the Valley of Death is neither simple nor easy (the authors highlight six key systems practitioners must navigate), they share the lessons they have learned in an easy to understand and engaging style that makes it accessible to both the novice and the expert alike. Individuals interested in successfully crossing the Valley of Death or guiding others will find an invaluable guide for making this journey. At the same time, innovation and entrepreneurship scholars interested in gaining a better understanding of how technology commercialization actually happens in the trenches will find this volume a nice addition to their library.

—Denis O. Gray, Ph.D, Alumni Distinguished Graduate Professor, Psychology in the Public Interest Program, Psychology Department, NC State University

Dedicated to the leaders who toil to innovate,
often without thanks or recognition.

CONTENTS

TABLE OF FIGURES

Maturity Model Definitions

Progression of Practices for the IMMA
Idea Management Competency

IMMA Heat Map

Sample Heat Map

TABLE OF WORKSHEETS

ACKNOWLEDGMENTS

The authors thank all the members and partners of the Center for Innovation Management Studies (CIMS). In a very real sense, this book is for them and organizations like them striving to master innovation.

Without their financial support and participation over the last four years, the research findings that define the System for Industrial Innovation would not have been possible. These members and partners, current and former, include:

Air Products & Chemicals

American Coatings Association

Armstrong World Industries

BASF

BP

Cisco Systems

Eastman Chemical

Eisai Pharmaceuticals

IBM

Kelly Services

Kenan Institute for Engineering, Technology & Science

MeadWestvaco (MWV)

National Science Foundation

NC Biotechnology Center

Novozymes North America

Pentair Water Pool and Spa

Pitney Bowes

Poole College of Management

Xerox

We would be remiss in not acknowledging the support and efforts of so many others, including:

Michelle Grainger, Managing Director for CIMS, who is the heart and soul of the organization. She managed the highly productive relationships between the innovation leaders and the research that created both the environment and opportunity to write this book.

Michael F. Wolff, who not only edited this book but is also the longtime editor of the CIMS newsletter, *The Innovation Management Report*. His insights into the content of this book are based on 25 years of experience as an award-winning editor of the journal *Research Technology Management*. He provided the authors with a constant stream of important ideas and suggestions.

Frederick Renk, our colleague and collaborator, who provided many helpful comments from the perspective of a distinguished scientist, product developer, and R&D executive.

Timothy Michaelis for research assistance and reference work throughout the project.

We also thank Suzanne M. Wood, who copyedited the book; Cyn Macgregor, who provided graphic design and production services; and Susan M. Katz, who proofread the book.

We acknowledge our debt to Alden Bean, the founder of the Center for Innovation Management Studies. Whose wisdom and encyclopedic knowledge of all things innovation continues to provide us with guidance and direction.

Finally we thank our wives Allyson and Carmen for their helpful guidance and keeping us headed in the right direction. They provided perspective, encouragement, and stability to complete this project.

FOREWORD

The book you hold in your hands takes up a big issue: Why do mature companies so often screw things up when it comes to driving growth through innovation? Why do these companies–full of bright engineers, creative marketers, seasoned managers, and lavishly-paid senior executives–get it wrong so often? Is this inevitable because innovation is so inherently difficult? Or is it the way we approach innovation that is woefully in need of transformation?

The authors of this book believe it is the latter. They offer, in these pages, a tested, proven, and comprehensive new approach that is sure to become the new hallmark of the Innovation Movement.

Authors Markham and Mugge have unimpeachable credibility to tackle this task. Both have vast industry experience. Both have seen countless successes and endless messes. Yet both have emerged unscathed and without cynicism. They do not shout their new method from the rooftops. They are not wild-eyed promoters. However, they are quiet revolutionaries, nonetheless, who promise to upend the current assumptions with a simple but compelling premise: *There is a better way to do innovation.* In this volume, they reveal it: systematic innovation.

Traversing the Valley of Death was written for innovation leaders. It will guide you in overcoming the barriers to commercializing growth-spawning projects. It is a full-on system, not a disjointed collection of random tools and best practices. It spans the entire innovation process: from idea generation and opportunity-sensing, through the development phase, and on through the internal Valley of Death by a thousand cuts (budget, resource allocation, etc.). It deals forthrightly with all the ways an idea can get derailed and arms you with tools to encourage you to think ahead of the curve. And it motivates you to get started!

Perhaps the biggest barrier to successful innovation is not risk-averse management, but a new threat: the sheer complexity of innovating in mind-numbingly large organizations. As the authors point out, the information requirements for big, radical projects are substantial. Thus, in Chapter 7, *Tools and Techniques*, the authors demonstrate how to integrate Big Data analytics to mitigate this numbing complexity and win with new projects.

What gives this book particular resonance is that both authors are affiliated with one of the top public-private innovation consortiums in the world: NC State University's Center for Innovation Management

Studies (CIMS). Think of it as a test laboratory for practitioners to come together in confidence to speak frankly about key issues within their companies. The Markham-Mugge system is thus constantly being tested at organizations such as IBM, BASF, Cisco, NetApp, Biogen Idec, Air Products, Kelly Services, MeadWestvaco, Pentair, and many others.

What they have given us in this volume is a step-by-step guide not just for avoiding the booby traps and snipers that lurk in that Valley of Death, but an inspiring treatise for delivering breakthrough products and services, stepping up your game, and becoming indispensable to your organization.

Robert B. Tucker

Santa Barbara, California

September 2014

Notes:

PREFACE

For those who have experienced it, the Valley of Death can be all too real. And crossing it may feel more like going over Niagara Falls in a barrel! After all, this is the place where good ideas go to die. This void—which separates the people engaged in research and discovery from those involved in commercializing their idea—is fraught with challenges. To start with, these people have different value systems, speak a different language, and, to top it all off, they don't always trust or respect each other. (Ever hear technical folks disparaged as "propeller heads" or noticed someone from the business end referred to as a "suit"?)

Referring to the activities that take place in this Valley as the fuzzy front end of innovation doesn't get it either. First of all, anything referred to as "fuzzy" is automatically a non-starter in today's boardrooms. These people want facts, not fuzz. Second, it leaves the impression that crossing the Valley of Death is nothing more than planned serendipity, controlled by luck and fate. Third, the fuzzy front end is the easy and fun part—it's the hairy back end that is hard and draining. The front end is only part of the problem.

We don't hold with any of these precepts. Yes, traversing the Valley of Death can be perilous (only 1 out of 10 ideas successfully make the crossing). But, in our opinion, this poor success rate is because Innovation Leaders—and their teams—are often ill-equipped for the journey. For these people—and their organizations—we offer the *CIMS*[1] *System for Industrial Innovation.*

Traversing the Valley of Death and managing major industrial innovation is the same thing.

Through a series of exercises and worksheets, the System (as we call it) helps organizations quickly develop ideas into legitimate, profitable, business opportunities and capture these opportunities in a compelling business case (the stuff the senior management of these organizations wants to see) in order to secure necessary resources. The System also

---

1. The Center for Innovation Management Studies (CIMS) is a unique industry-academia partnership that makes its home in the Poole College of Management at NC State University in Raleigh, NC. Its members are the Who's Who of American industry. For more than 30 years, these organizations have set the CIMS research agenda, investigating every facet of innovation management.

recommends the crucial governance system and metrics required to implement them. In other words, the System lays out an entire strategy and tool kit for crossing the Valley of Death.

The System for Industrial Innovation is not a theoretical construct or some academic exercise. As we write this, it has already been put into practice at more than a dozen companies, including large ones such as IBM, BP, Cisco, Novozymes, MeadWestvaco, Bayer, Eisai Pharmaceuticals, Air Products and Chemicals, Biogen Idec, Kelly Services, Nortel, Kobe Steel, and Eastman Chemical and smaller companies such as NetApp, Pentair, and Bell and Howell. We have deployed it at startup companies such as LipoScience Inc., Kyma Technologies, Premitech, Veritasand, and LipsInc. It is also used by other universities and governmental and international agencies, such as The Ohio State University, Loughborough University in England, Hanbat University in South Korea, NASA, the Kenan Institute, Portugal's Technology Commercialization Program and South Korea's Innopolis.

Moreover, our writing has been informed by 20 years of research and practice in managing innovation here at NC State, as described below, as well as our combined 60-plus years in industry. This includes Paul Mugge's 35 years in product development, global business strategy, and business innovation services at IBM and Steve Markham's experiences consulting with numerous Fortune 500 companies, starting more than 20 high-tech companies, and serving others in roles such as board member, CEO, CFO, COO, VP of product development, equity investor, and managing director.

The System's Roots Go Deep

The roots of the System go back 20 years to when Professors Stephen Markham, Angus Kingon, Michael Zapata, Gary Palin, James Jeck, David Baumer, Lynda Aiman-Smith, Karlyn Mitchell, and Cecil Bozarth introduced what is called the TEC Algorithm, which continues to be developed with Markham, Steve Barr, Ted Baker, Raj Narayan, and Roger Debo. The term TEC (Technology Education and Commercialization) was coined by Jerry Cuomo, Distinguished Research Professor at the College of Engineering, NC State University, who suggested students should graduate into their own companies.

Funded by the National Science Foundation (NSF) and the Kenan Institute for Engineering, Technology and Science, as well as generous corporate sponsors, the TEC Algorithm was and still is the backbone of the Poole College of Management's entrepreneurship program. Its use has led to the launch of scores of successful ventures, the generation of more than $270 million in venture funding, the employment of 500-plus people, and the introduction of 60 products to market on four continents. It serves as a formidable base on which to build the System.

The tools and techniques used in the System have been in continual development throughout the past 20 years. Dr. Markham has tested them successfully in multiple MBA courses, including Global Strategy, Management of Technology and Innovation, and Building Business Models. More than 50 companies have employed many of these tools, and their feedback has allowed us to continuously refine the System.

Additional points that bear emphasizing here:

- Our focus is on what we call Big Innovation—true breakthrough innovation, rather than the incrementalism that has led too many of today's large companies to the commoditization of their products and services.

- A system is necessary for breakthrough innovation because large-scale, disruptive innovation affects the entire organization. Isolated innovation projects rarely command attention in mature organizations, particularly those driven by operational efficiency.

In a very real sense, the System helps "de-risk" breakthrough innovation. Applied in the manner our handbook prescribes, it can help you make the bets that lead to Big Innovation.

How the Book Is Organized

Although it may sound like one, *Traversing the Valley of Death* is not an adventure novel. It is first and foremost a handbook for busy Innovation Leaders. Consequently, we are offering the book in a number of formats—as a classic hardbound business book, in paperback, and as an e-book that you can read on your Kindle or iPad. We designed the book to go with you wherever you go. You can take it to meetings with you, you can read it while waiting in airports or crammed into your airline seat, or you can delve into it late at night in the comfort of your home. Who said crossing the Valley of Death was going to be a 9-to-5 job?

Within the framework of a conventional book, we include a workbook that contains more than 30 worksheets and exercises that teams need to actually manage and produce breakthrough innovations. The worksheets are the jewels of the System. But they are not meant to be dogmatically filled in. Rather, they are designed to engender thinking—and discussion—around the critical factors facing the project. Although each worksheet builds on the worksheet before it, we encourage flexibility. A project team that is confident about what it has accomplished—and confident about what it should do next—can go directly to whatever worksheet is most relevant.

Big Innovation is never a single event, nor does it travel in a straight line. Instead, it is an ongoing, iterative process of turning smart ideas into actionable business cases.

Chapter 1, *Introduction*, describes the primary audience for this handbook: Innovation Leaders. These are the highly talented and dedicated people charged with leading their organizations' perpetual pursuit of new, differentiated, and profitable products and services. The chapter also explains why the System is intended for mature or established companies, which for a variety of reasons must overcome increasingly difficult challenges, like strategic diffusion and complacency forged by years of success. While these companies have the capacity to properly assess and develop new market opportunities, they often take shortcuts with Big Innovation projects, only to see them crash in the Valley of Death.

Chapter 2, *Foundations of Industrial Innovation*, lays out in more depth the basic framework that underlies breakthrough innovation: the Valley of Death. It also describes the pioneering efforts that went into creating the TEC Algorithm, the first successful process for crossing that Valley. The Algorithm's method for connecting ideas to products to markets with enduring customer needs is the essence of breakthrough innovation—and the System for Industrial Innovation. The chapter concludes with the five dimensions into which the TEC Algorithm has been extended to meet the formidable new challenges confronting Innovation Leaders today.

Chapter 3, *A System for Industrial Innovation*, introduces the six subsystems that comprise the overall System and the three modules into which they are organized (see illustration).

System for Industrial Innovation

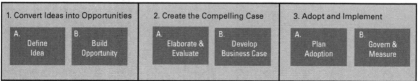

1. Convert Ideas into Opportunities		2. Create the Compelling Case		3. Adopt and Implement	
A. Define Idea	B. Build Opportunity	A. Elaborate & Evaluate	B. Develop Business Case	A. Plan Adoption	B. Govern & Measure

Each module constitutes a principal step in the innovation process: Convert Ideas into Opportunities, Create the Compelling Case, and Adopt and Implement. In this way, the chapter provides an overview of the entire process and the governance system (roles and responsibilities, decision authorities, and metrics) required to embed it within your organization.

We also explain the philosophy that guided the System's construction, as well as the way in which we employ Big Data analytics tools to gather, filter, and present information in ways never before possible. Breakthrough innovation is all about making substantial bets on sometimes uncertain market opportunities. These tools can give Innovation Leaders and their organizations the confidence to do just that.

Chapters 4, 5, and 6 explain the three modules and six subsystems of the System in detail. In Chapter 4, *Module 1: Convert Ideas into Opportunities*, you will learn what it takes to define an idea and then develop it into a true business opportunity. Chapter 5, *Module 2: Create the Compelling Case*, advances the process by explaining how to elaborate on and evaluate that opportunity and develop a business case (not a business plan) that is grounded in enduring customer needs and your company's ability to deliver it. Chapter 6, *Module 3: Adopt and Implement*, lays out the final two steps in the process: getting your opportunity adopted inside the organization and measuring the capacity of the organization to repeatedly and systematically do breakthrough innovation.

In addition to presenting a holistic approach to crossing the Valley of Death, these chapters provide users with a complete toolbox of decision-support tools. They make up what we call the workbook of *Traversing the Valley of Death*. All of the tools and worksheets are available online at www.TraversingTheValleyOfDeath.com.

While the tone of Chapters 1, 2, and 3 is more conversational, Chapters 4, 5, and 6 are more instructional and prescriptive by design. These chapters contain a series of worksheets that help guide Innovation Leaders and teams through the Valley of Death. By gathering and assessing only the necessary information—and filling in their workbook before proceeding to the next step—users are sure to adhere to the System's recommended workflow. Also, using the workbook in this fashion memorializes the entire project for subsequent review and learning.

Finally, Chapter 7, *Tools and Techniques*, provides, as a bonus to readers, a more in-depth explanation of Big Data and other tools and techniques needed to fully implement breakthrough innovation. These topics are too large to include in the heart of the handbook (Chapters 4-6), but should be applied as needed to fully realize the potential of the System.

We are confident that after reading this handbook, leaders of industrial organizations—and the teams they mobilize—will have a much better understanding of what it takes to create truly unique and differentiated offerings for their customers. Moreover, if they follow the proven path we have laid out for them, they will be able to do this in less time, using fewer resources, and with a far greater chance of success.

Final Thought

If this is your organization's first attempt at traversing the Valley of Death, it will seem like a high-wire act. But if you follow the guidance we put forward, with repeated application it will begin to feel more like a four-lane highway bridge. We promise.

To help get you started fast, visit our website for a complete set of tools, application tips, and advice from experienced users:

www.TraversingTheValleyOfDeath.com

Notes:

CHAPTER 1.

Introduction

Innovation Leaders Are Central

This handbook is intended primarily for managers charged with dramatically changing their organization's top-line performance. At the Center for Innovation Management Studies (CIMS), we call these people Innovation Leaders. Position and title do not define these people; they may, or may not, hold the title of Chief Innovation Officer. They may just as likely be found at the business unit or functional level: Strategic Business Unit General Manager, Head of R&D, Business Development, Marketing, and so on. In some cases, Innovation Leaders can be self-appointed. In fact, we believe that innovation is everyone's responsibility.

Innovation Leaders are usually seasoned, influential executives. While we have great respect for mid-level managers and idea champions at all levels, it is our experience that it is almost impossible to lead major innovation programs from these ranks.

But more important than their position in the organization are the traits Innovation Leaders possess:

- They don't review innovation initiatives, but rather roll up their sleeves and spend a good portion of their time working with innovation project teams and potential customers to understand first hand the needs and wants of these customers.

- Drawing on their experience, they can gauge when a product in development will be more profitable if they convert it to a service opportunity. They can spot an unmet need during the business-model building process, and they have the stature to change course and pursue the better opportunity.

- Innovation Leaders are team players; they are generally inclusive and respectful of others, particularly their peers. Because of the respect they engender, they can quickly mobilize resources across the organization.

- They have a clear view of what is in, or out, of alignment in terms of skills and capabilities, metrics and incentives, and how well people are collaborating in order to get the most from their collective efforts.

- Most importantly, Innovation Leaders are decisive. If an opportunity cannot prove itself after a reasonable amount of time, they kill it—thereby freeing resources for other projects in the portfolio.

CIMS serves Innovation Leaders; they set the research agenda. And they play a central role in the CIMS System for Industrial Innovation (the System). They help form and gather resources for the organization's principal innovation management function, which we call the innovation portfolio committee and describe in Chapter 6, *Module 3: Adopt and Implement.* Most importantly, these leaders have the authority to launch projects that address opportunities and fill gaps in the company's business portfolio.

As we can attest from more than 30 years observing these unusually valuable people, they do not seek silver bullets. Just the opposite: they want solutions that will last. They are willing to take the time to study, plan, design, and implement a robust innovation program for their organizations. They are determined that innovation be treated neither as a fad nor a luxury, but as a necessity to be embedded firmly within their organization's DNA.

If this describes you, or someone you aspire to be, we welcome you on this journey.

Mature Companies Have the Toughest Task

This book focuses on mature or established companies. These firms are often at least one level of customer removed from their end user. In other words, the people who buy their products are not necessarily the same as the people who use these products on a regular basis. Hence, these firms have more difficulty seeing, understanding, and profiting from the opportunities new markets present.

In addition, these companies typically rely on third-party reports to build estimates of their market size and segments of buyers within their market. But because such companies lack both an intimate relationship with end users and a deep understanding of the needs of those users, they often find these definitions so general as to be all but useless for creating profitable new products.

Compounding the problem, large, mature companies typically serve multiple masters—in other words, many different customers with different needs. For example, IBM sells computers and services to financial institutions, automotive companies, pharmaceutical firms, local and federal governments, and so on, ranging from huge user communities to very small ones. So executives at companies like IBM must ask themselves: Which industry and end-user customer segment is the right focus for deep, profitable relations? Which markets should we excel at serving?

Strategic Diffusion

Large, mature firms often suffer from strategic diffusion. Simply expressed, strategic diffusion is too many complex strategic battles being fought at the same time. Research by the Corporate Executive Board shows an alarming number of case history companies were suffering from strategic diffusion well before revenues flattened and their stock price took a beating (1).

Strategic diffusion can show itself in two forms:

- In multi-industry conglomerates, management teams are engaged in strategic confrontations across a broad front of dissimilar businesses. These companies often extend management across too many industries, thereby stretching strategic control too thin. As a result, they often wake up to find multiple businesses turning down at the same time.

- Too many strategic initiatives are launched simultaneously within the same or similar business in an effort to solve everything at once. Management teams dilute their efforts and their execution across too many activities (2).

Regardless of the form strategic diffusion takes, several common, damaging symptoms reveal themselves in the portfolios of these firms. They are crammed with too many projects and too few winners. The cycle time of the development projects is lengthening, not shortening, as the struggle for an ever-thinning set of engineering resources rises. And the execution and quality of the projects suffer, causing even more re-dos and delays.

Another symptom of strategic diffusion is the increasing number of failed projects. Before these projects are even completed, the opportunity has passed them by and the only recourse is to cancel them, although even this may be beyond the abilities of a strategically diffused organization. It has no better reason for killing a project than it did for selecting the project in the first place (3).

The worst outcome of strategic diffusion is the toll it takes on the organization's business performance. Unless executives are just plain lucky, a strategically diffused organization will never achieve its business objectives.

Success Breeds Complacency

Having been successful for a number of years, many mature companies now view breakthrough innovations—major innovations that are new to the world, or at least to their industry—as too risky. That risk manifests itself in many ways, but usually the first one expressed is that the financial returns from such initiatives, if any, are realized too far in the future.

Mature companies often fall captive to Wall Street and seek to constantly post quarterly results that beat estimates. The risk of the familiar seems small; the risk of the new, too large.

Consequently, such firms can fall victim to what we call the "stuck-in-incrementalism" syndrome, undertaking only small changes. What innovations they do produce tend to be incremental in nature— essentially, extensions or derivatives of their current product or service platforms. Of course, this aversion to taking a risk and pursuing breakthrough innovation can only lead to one outcome: the inevitable commoditization of their products and services, followed by declining margins and stagnant growth.

We believe that all organizations should devote some portion of their portfolios to breakthrough initiatives that seek to create whole, new competitive platforms—and new potential sources of revenue growth. Although the resource allotment dedicated to breakthrough initiatives will vary depending on the industry, every company must set aside some resources to explore more radical ideas.

We understand that derivations based on existing product and service platforms can be profitable from a time-to-market standpoint for reinforcing a company's brand value and for creating significant economic benefits for the firm. Project portfolios must contain both incremental and breakthrough innovation projects in order to be balanced from a risk/return standpoint.

This book defines the ability of organizations to create an entire stream of profitable products from a set of core components and competencies as platform management. Trouble occurs when these platforms start becoming obsolete or when companies try to force them into market segments they were not designed for.

The Need for New Metrics

It is important for companies to use different metrics for the breakthrough portions of their portfolios. For their incremental innovations, mature businesses usually measure planned and actual increases in unit volumes, revenue, and earnings in relation to their P&L plans. However, these metrics are not useful for measuring the progress of early-stage breakthrough initiatives. They may even undermine breakthrough innovation efforts.

In contrast, breakthrough initiatives should employ metrics that track progress in identifying and understanding customers' problems and learning how to solve them. Measures might include the number of interactions per month between senior management and customers; the team's success in rapidly creating prototypes for early feedback; the results of market tests; the volume and nature of customer complaints about the product, from the introduction of the initial prototype onward; and the team's ability to respond to those complaints (4). (For more about the importance of portfolio management and metrics to managing breakthrough innovations, see Chapter 6, *Module 3: Adopt and Implement.*)

Getting the All-Important Market Concept Right

As noted, mature companies have a particularly hard time seeing the market. Yet we know that a company's ability to crystallize the market concept—the target segment and how the company's offerings can do a better job of meeting the customer's needs—is even more important than how well the company fields a fundamentally new product or technology. In fact, research by Procter & Gamble suggests that 70 percent of product failures across most categories occur because companies misconstrue the market (5).

New Coke is a classic market concept failure by an existing mature firm; in contrast, Netflix got its market concept right (6). In each case the outcome was determined by the company's understanding of the market, not its facility with the enabling technologies. But it was likely easier for a startup like Netflix, which didn't have to carry the burdens of past practice.

Moreover, establishing the nature of the market can head off a costly technology push. This overdone strategy often afflicts companies that emphasize how to solve a problem rather than what problem should be solved or what customer desires must be satisfied (7). Sometimes, a simpler solution, rather than more technology, is the right answer.

The solution for Innovation Leaders in both mature businesses as well as startup firms is a systematic process—complete with proven tools and techniques—that will help them recognize and quantify new market opportunities.

Key decision points in the System employ the emerging discipline of Big Data analytics to provide the information executives need to make the hard decisions associated with risky, breakthrough innovations.

The solution must also foster an organizational spirit of entrepreneurship that large, mature firms often lack (8). While we know that many mature companies' business models have been optimized for operational excellence, they must still take on some risk and look beyond quarterly results if they wish to reignite their growth engines. They are also finding it increasingly necessary to look beyond the boundaries of their own organization for partners able to co-create these new products and ventures, share the risk, and provide much needed expertise.

REFERENCES FOR CHAPTER 1

1. Corporate Executive Board. 2006. "Overcoming Stall Points: New Frameworks for Recognizing and Responding to Growth Pitfalls." White paper, accessed July 2014. https://csb.executiveboard.com/OvercomingStallPointsPrintable.pdf.

2. O'Neill, H.M., Pouder, R.W., and Buchholtz, A.K. 1998. "Patterns in the Diffusion of Strategies across Organizations: Insights from the Innovation Diffusion Literature." *Academy of Management Review*, 23: 98-114.

3. Abrahamson, E. 1991. "Managerial Fads and Fashions: The Diffusion and Rejection of Innovations." *Academy of Management Review*, 16: 586-612.

4. Laurie, D.L., and Harreld, B. 2013. "Six Ways to Sink a Growth Initiative." *Harvard Business Review*, 91: 82-90.

5. Dodgson, M., Gann, D., and Salter, A. 2006. "The Role of Technology in the Shift Toward Open Innovation: The Case of Procter & Gamble." *R&D Management*, 36: 333-346.

6. Schindler, R.M. 1992. "The Real Lesson of New Coke: The Value of Focus Groups for Predicting the Effects of Social Influence." *Marketing Research*, May: 22-27.

7. Day, G.S. 2007. "Is It Real? Can We Win? Is It Worth It?" 2007. *Harvard Business Review*, 85:110-120.

8. Ahuja, G., and Lampert, C.M. 2001. "Entrepreneurship in the Large Corporation: A Longitudinal Study of How Established Firms Create Breakthrough Inventions." *Strategic Management Journal*, 22: 521-543.

Notes:

CHAPTER 2.

Foundations of Industrial Innovation

Valley of Death

We begin by examining how breakthrough innovation occurs—and what often kills it. Although most companies realize innovation is the key to maintaining a competitive advantage and growth, they constantly struggle to convert new, breakthrough ideas into products and services. A major reason is that bringing new ideas to market is not a seamless process. Multiple factors contribute to this struggle, including social, political, and cultural forces as well as limitations on people, money, and other resources, plus the sheer limits on knowledge. These barriers to innovation occur frequently during the dangerous interval between discovery and commercialization.

In between the relatively well-defined activities of discovery and commercialization lies the more nebulous phase called the "Valley of Death" (Fig. 2-1). The Valley is a vague, poorly-defined decision space devoted to converting ideas to opportunities, developing a compelling business case, and adopting and implementing the new idea (1, 2, 3). Discovery activities, on the left side of the Valley, include basic scientific research, macro-environment trend analysis, technology development and prototyping, Voice of the Customer, and so forth. Activities necessary to commercialize an idea, on the right side of the Valley, include new product and services development, industrial design, manufacturing, product management (pricing, positioning, forecasting, and promotion), as well as sales and marketing and customer support.

Valley of Death: The Space Connecting Ideas to Markets

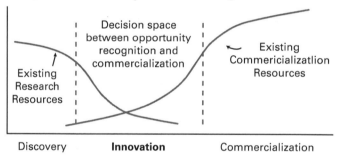

Figure 2-1. The Valley of Death is where most ideas disappear.

Key Roles – Champions, Sponsors, and Gatekeepers

Three players lead the decisions required to cross the Valley: Champions, Sponsors, and Gatekeepers (4, 5). The Champions' major contribution is recognizing the value of the idea, then "selling" it to Sponsors who possess the resources needed to demonstrate the viability to Gatekeepers. Gatekeepers are the people with the decision authority over access to resources and who accept and support projects for further development. (See Fig. 2-2.)

Interaction and Integration Are Key

Much of the literature describing the roles of Champion, Sponsor, and Gatekeeper assumes that they remain static throughout the entire innovation process, from idea to commercialization. Little research has examined how roles might change and interact as the innovation process progresses.

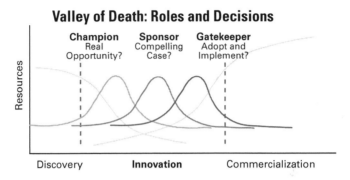

Figure 2-2. Decision roles will change dramatically over a project's life.

A notable exception is Drazin and Van de Ven, who found that activity levels among different role holders vary dramatically over the life of a project (6). Other researchers have noted that roles throughout this innovation process are likely to be linked, and those playing these roles coordinate their efforts (7). We suggest that these three roles must interact to cross the Valley of Death. For example, the Champion who finds and advocates for a project will seek out Sponsors who will decide whether to support the project. The Champion depends on the Sponsor for support, and the Sponsor depends on the Champion for good opportunities.

Similarly, after developing and supporting a project, the Champion and Sponsor will try to get the project approved by the Gatekeeper for further development.

Value Systems Not Aligned

Further impeding interactions is the fact that the people on either side of the Valley have different value systems. Their formal education, objectives, measurements, rewards, and recognition diverge, sometimes dramatically. And, if not in direct conflict, they are certainly not aligned. Discovery-oriented scientists in universities may have little familiarity with business realities and cost constraints, for instance.

Even within a given business, tensions between the discovery and commercial sides run high and are well documented (see, for example,

8,9,10). Roberts observes, "Most large firms are deficient in bringing the marketing vice president and marketing organization...into a compatible and parallel role with the CTO..." (11). Roberts notes similar gaps between chief financial officers and the head of the R&D business units. The parties speak different languages, value different outcomes, and often do not consult with one another in ways that might reconcile these differences. The result is failed innovation.

Implications

Not only have we studied the Valley of Death, we have actually performed the roles of Champion, Sponsor, and Gatekeeper during our industrial careers. We know that without a systematic process, crossing the Valley of Death will remain a perilous, ad hoc endeavor dependent upon the persistence of the Champion, the patience of the Sponsor, the resources of the Gatekeeper—and a good bit of luck. We also know that breakthrough ideas place an added stress on an organization already divided in its business goals and values.

Consequently, to master crossing the Valley of Death will require a new, transparent governance structure and culture, one that integrates the decisions of the Champion, Sponsor, and Gatekeeper along with those of other key stakeholders in the organization. "New," because such integration is not the norm. "Transparent," because the sunlight of shared information and common metrics is essential to enable the integration that will reduce risk and increase trust among those who must collaborate to achieve the goal.

The Valley of Death then offers a unifying framework for breakthrough innovation, and crossing it is the objective of the System.

TEC Renaissance

In 2010, CIMS members launched a new, multi-year investigation into breakthrough innovation. The objective of the research program, code named TEC Renaissance, was to update and expand the older, highly successful TEC Algorithm to address the global competitive pressures that mature companies experience today. In addition, the TEC Renaissance would take advantage of the vastly more powerful information technology available to innovation leaders. (For a list of CIMS members who sponsored this research, see the Acknowledgements.)

History of the TEC Algorithm

The TEC Algorithm is the backbone of the Poole College of Management's graduate degree program in entrepreneurship and has been used by faculty and students for 18 years. Originally funded by grants from the National Science Foundation and the Kenan Institute for Engineering, Technology and Science, it was the first methodology that offered a series of highly structured commercialization tools designed specifically to help firms cross the Valley of Death.

During the past 18 years the TEC Algorithm has been used to evaluate more than 1,150 technologies. It has also helped raise $270 million in venture funding to start new companies based on business plans developed in the program, created more than 500 jobs, and initiated dozens of technology licenses. At the same time, NC State faculty introduced the TEC Algorithm into companies such as Becton Dickenson, Nortel, BP, Kobe Steel, Motorola, MeadWestvaco, and universities elsewhere in the United States, including The Ohio State University, California Polytechnic, and Brown University. We also took TEC to universities in Portugal, Slovenia, England, Korea, and South Africa.

For companies and universities desiring to be more entrepreneurial, the TEC Algorithm provides a great place to start, with abundant past experience to guide the way.

How the Algorithm Works

The key construct used to generate and capture lots of ideas is called "CPM," which refers to "Capability–Product–Market" linkages (see Fig. 2-3). An example of the use of CPM with students can help explain how CPM works. Interdisciplinary teams, composed of students from the Colleges of Engineering, Sciences, Textiles, Design, as well as students from the College of Management, are asked to trace the path that connects specific capabilities (C), through potential product concepts (P), to the needs of customers in a particular market segment (M). They are then instructed to find additional market needs the product could satisfy or to propose a new product enabled by the technology. This process continues—iterating between technological capabilities, specific product features, and genuine market needs—until a robust and prioritized commercialization strategy for the technology or capability has been identified.

Capability - Product - Market Linkages

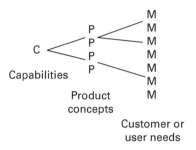

Figure 2-3. Capability-Product-Market linkages underpin a robust commercialization strategy.

For example, students recently applied CPM to a single patented chemical compound to describe product ideas as diverse as a fluid that prolongs the useful life of transplant organs, an anti-aging skin cream, and an energy drink. To map the CPM linkages, the team was guided through intense sessions and encouraged to focus only on what is "knowable and discriminating." Identifying diverse market needs guides the process of further specifying product attributes and—if the initial technology appears incomplete or inadequate—the search for further technologies with the needed performance characteristics. In the end, the teams (whether students or industry executives) are able to articulate not just one Capability-Product-Market linkage, but rather an entire array of possibilities: a product platform that is prioritized according to the wants and needs of specific markets (12).

The TEC Algorithm is developmental, not evaluative. Evaluation and selection are deferred until the product ideas are fully developed. In fact, both students and companies are told to cease expensive technology development until the linkages to real market needs can be supported with facts. Technologists who learn this important lesson can never think of their technology development activities in the same way again.

Rather than performing more and more experimentation, they start thinking of the specific technology capability they will need to demonstrate in order to create a product that satisfies the documented wants and needs of customers.

The CPM construct allows its users to begin with a capability, but move quickly to understanding the decisive role in commercialization of product and market forces, thereby effectively integrating technology push and market pull logics.

New Requirements for the System

As practical and successful as the TEC Algorithm continues to be, new tools and techniques have been developed. More important, macro-market trends—such as the rising market power of emerging economies, sustainability of the planet's resources, customers' increasing desire for total solutions, and the transition of companies toward open and collaborative business models—invite a refreshed and updated design for the TEC Algorithm.

Specifically, the TEC Renaissance extended the TEC Algorithm in five dimensions:

Service Innovation. Many more companies today offer both goods and services to their customers. CIMS-funded research in collaboration with the Product Development and Management Association (PDMA) found that service innovation takes a distinctly different path from that of goods development and requires a different mindset and practices (13). The System incorporates the latest services-development knowledge.

Early-Stage Market Research. A primary limitation on early commercialization is faulty understanding of the potential markets for products that do not yet exist. Recent development in natural language analytics can be used to identify segments and define potential market needs. The ability to make informed, cogent decisions by gathering, filtering, annotating, and displaying massive amounts of data—by anyone trained in this method—represents a paradigm shift and extraordinary potential unavailable just a decade ago. Current knowledge of trends that promise both threats and opportunities to an organization, of new technological advances and where they are occurring, and of potential business partners to exploit these opportunities offer great promise for supercharging an organization's capacity to innovate and grow. The new System combines a capability for early market description with the TEC Algorithm's evaluation process to find new markets and applications for new technologies, as well as potential partners, by using Big Data analytics.

Global Scope. Technology commercialization is an intensely global activity. The commercial viability of a new technology-based product or service often requires a global perspective to understand the application and uses. Although some companies do incorporate global thinking in product development, this is difficult to do at the very earliest stages, when the full range of applications has not yet been explored. The TEC Renaissance program developed a systematic process for incorporating global thinking at the earliest stages of ideation. Moreover, the computer-based nature of inquiry permits rapid updating as new questions arise.

Open Innovation. We know from studying breakthrough innovation that many breakthrough ideas often come from outside the boundaries of the firm (14). With respect to the Valley of Death, this means the entire set of discovery activities may be conducted outside the company, with key business partners, universities, small startups, and others. In 2000, in an effort to increase top-line sales, Alan G. Lafley, CEO of Procter & Gamble, ordered that 50 percent of P&G's new products be based on ideas that were generated from outside the firm (15). His strategy wasn't to replace the capabilities of P&G's 7,500 researchers and support staff, but to better leverage them. Half of P&G's new products now arise from outside the firm. But simply finding new ideas is insufficient. Success requires an innovation strategy, changed governance structures, and an innovation-friendly culture, no matter the business model or source of new ideas. The TEC Renaissance program incorporates this new insight.

Adoption. Perhaps the most difficult part of commercializing a new technology is the adoption of a new product internally, particularly for more breakthrough initiatives. Teams are likely to react, "This is not the way we do things around here!" The process by which more innovative projects find internal support is not well understood and often results in high-potential projects dying before they ever reach the market. The best practices for internal adoption of radical new products begin with a central issue: preparing a business case suitable for managerial decision-making. The System incorporates business-case thinking from the outset, enhancing the market understanding of technologists as well as the technology understanding of marketers.

REFERENCES FOR CHAPTER 2

1. Auerswald, P.E., and Branscomb, L.M. 2003. "Valleys of Death and Darwinian Seas: Financing the Invention to Innovation Transition in the United States." *The Journal of Technology Transfer*, 28: 227-239.

2. Markham, S.K. 2002. "Moving Technologies from Lab to Market." *Research-Technology Management*, 45: 31-42.

3. Merrifield, B.D. 1995. "Obsolescence of Core Competencies Versus Corporate Renewal." *Technology Management*, 2: 73–83.

4. Howell, J.M., and Higgins, C.A. 1990. "Champions of Technological Innovation." *Administrative Science Quarterly*, 35: 317-341.

5. Markham, S.K., and Griffin, A. 1998. "The Breakfast of Champions: Associations between Champions and Product Development Environments, Practices and Performance." *Journal of Product Innovation Management*, 15: 436-454.

6. Drazin, R., and Van de Ven, A.H. 1985. "Alternative Forms of Fit in Contingency Theory." *Administrative Science Quarterly*, 30: 514-539.

7. Utterback, J.M. 1971. "The Process of Technological Innovation within the Firm." *Academy of Management Journal*, 14: 75-88.

8. Fisher, R.J., Maltz, E., and Jaworski, B.J. 1997. "Enhancing Communication between Marketing and Engineering: The Moderating Role of Relative Functional Identification." *The Journal of Marketing*, 61: 54-70.

9. Gupta, A.K., Raj, S.P., and Wilemon, D. 1986. "A Model for Studying R&D: Marketing Interface in the Product Innovation Process." *The Journal of Marketing*, 50: 7-17.

10. Souder, W.E. 1988. "Managing Relations between R&D and Marketing in New Product Development Projects." *Journal of Product Innovation Management*, 5: 6-19.

11. Roberts, E.B. 2004. "Linkage, Leverage and Leadership Drive Successful Technological Innovation." *Research-Technology Management*, 47: 9-11.

12. Barr, S.H., Baker, T., Markham, S.K., and Kingon, A.I. 2009. "Bridging the Valley of Death: Lessons Learned from 14 Years of Commercialization of Technology Education." *Academy of Management Learning & Education*, 8: 370-388.

13. Markham, S.K., and Holmann, T. 2012. "The Difference between Goods and Services Development: A PDMA CPAS Research Study." *PDMA Handbook of Product Development*, 3rd Edition. K. Khan and S. Uban (Eds). Wiley and Sons, Hoboken, New Jersey.

14. Reid, S.E., and De Brentani, U. 2004. "The Fuzzy Front End of New Product Development for Discontinuous Innovations: A Theoretical Model." *Journal of Product Innovation Management*, 21: 170-184.

15. Huston, L., and Sakkab, N. 2006. "P&G's New Innovation Model." *Harvard Business Review*, 84: 58-66.

Notes:

CHAPTER 3

A System for Industrial Innovation

A Process

Put simply, the System converts ideas into innovation. Its purpose is threefold: (1) To guide organizations to quickly develop ideas into legitimate, profitable business opportunities, (2) to capture these opportunities in a compelling case for securing the necessary resources, and (3) to plan for the adoption of the innovation and to establish the necessary governance system required to systematically do breakthrough innovation and measure the performance of that innovation in the marketplace. In other words, the System lays out an entire business system and strategy for actually doing breakthrough innovation.

System for Industrial Innovation

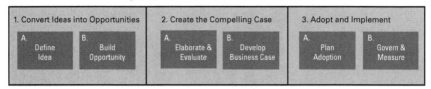

Figure 3-1. Six subsystems comprise the CIMS System for Industrial Innovation.

The six subsystems are organized in three modules, each divided into two components (Fig. 3-1) and constituting a principal step in the overall process of breakthrough innovation. We briefly introduce them here in Chapter 3 and then describe them in detail in Chapters 4, 5, and 6. In addition to providing a holistic approach to breakthrough innovation, these chapters provide users with a complete toolbox of innovation decision tools.

Each module is designed to progress the innovation to certain levels of maturity. In *Module 1A: Define the Idea*, the innovation is conducted by unassigned people in an ad hoc fashion but ends with a defined idea. As the innovation progresses into *Module 1B: Build the Opportunity*, a temporary team further defines the opportunity. Once the business opportunity is defined and approved, it enters into *Module 2A: Elaborate and Evaluate* and a permanent Innovation Project Team is officially assigned to manage what becomes a project. The Innovation Project Team continues to manage the project through *Module 2B: Develop the Business Case*. In *Module 3A: Plan Adoption*, the team leverages the value of the project as it plans for its adoption by the rest of organization. Finally, the team optimizes the project by carrying out the activities in *Module 3B: Govern and Measure*.

The System also embraces a number of key concepts that pervade the entire process. These are discussed below. Their understanding and mastery are important to properly implementing the System.

The System for Industrial Innovation

Module 1: Convert Ideas into Opportunities

Subsystem 1A: Define Idea

An "idea" is a conception recognized as likely to have commercial value.

An "opportunity" is an idea embedded in an enduring customer need and in the company's ability to deliver it to the market.

Having an idea is like having children–they are fun to conceive but hard to deliver! Ideas often come in a flash of entrepreneurial insight that something has commercial value. This is always an exhilarating experience. The problem is that most companies have more ideas than they have the ability, or capability, to deliver. In fact, most companies are awash in ideas: they have so many that they clog the organization's decision-making apparatus. With so many choices, they are unable to focus on a clear objective and must search blindly for the best idea.

The irony is that even when a company is choked with ideas, their management calls for more. They schedule ideation sessions, pull busy people into brainstorming sessions, and generate many more ideas that only choke the organization's decision-making further. Starved of decision-making oxygen, the decision makers' eyes dim with decisional apraxia.

The problem is not the lack of ideas, but the lack of real business opportunities.

The *Define Idea* step in Module 1 provides a series of tools that help users turn their fledgling ideas into well-thought-out and detailed business concepts. These tools force teams to answer questions such as: Why and how is this idea different? What benefits will it deliver to the organization and its customers? What makes it believable?

This is where most ideation systems break down. In the Valley of Death, this job usually falls on Champions. They have the cognitive skills that allow them to intuit new opportunities. But this can actually work to their detriment in large, established companies with entrenched development systems (1). In these firms, Gatekeepers and Sponsors alike want to know exactly where the idea is headed and what it will do for the firm. The System is designed to provide others in the organization with enough rationale and evidence to make informed resources decisions.

Subsystem 1B: Build Opportunity

For our purposes, a raw idea is the recognition that something has commercial value. Nevertheless, ideas are a dime a dozen. Opportunities are different—very different.

For an idea to be a business opportunity the idea must be embedded in (1) enduring customer needs and in (2) your company's ability to deliver it. Although this sounds deceptively simple, our research reveals that these are really the only two conditions that matter in the early stages of innovation.

The purpose of the *Build Opportunity* step is to refine your new ideas in terms of these imperatives to establish that they, in fact, represent a realistic business opportunity for the company.

Build Opportunity provides users with a set of proven tools that help them articulate the market needs as well as the abilities the organization needs to possess in order to satisfy these needs. The strength of this linkage, in large part, will determine the likelihood that the full potential of the idea will be realized.

Perhaps the hardest task facing Innovation Project Teams is to understand and prioritize the wants and needs of the customers. In other words, to help the team get the market concept right. The tools help identify and qualify both articulated and unarticulated market needs. Articulated needs are those needs that the target customers or users are able to state clearly enough for the developer to derive a product description. Techniques such as direct inquiry, Delphi, nominal group techniques, brainstorming, and discussion prompts can help people articulate their needs.

Unarticulated needs are those needs that the intended customer/users are unable to state clearly, often because a new technology or service lies outside their experience base. Early-stage market research techniques, like Voice of the Customer, trend analysis, technology scouting, and a variety of open innovation techniques, help users identify—and qualify—those latent needs.

To facilitate the use of these tools, we automate them with Big Data analytics. (See Big Data Analytics for Big Decisions, below.) The application of advanced analytics at this point in the process can prove a game changer. It gathers hard-to-obtain information and generates market intelligence at a rate and scale that would previously have been unaffordable, if not impossible.

Build Opportunity ends with the construction of the opportunity's value proposition and placing it with the other opportunities being developed by the organization in the initial *Opportunity Portfolio*.

It takes a lot of work to convert an idea into a business opportunity. We like to say, "Ideas are made, not born." Module 1 ensures that the idea is well defined and articulated to the point where it can be made actionable.

Module 2: Create the Compelling Case

After an idea has been worked into a business opportunity in Module 1 and opportunities have been prioritized, it's time to prepare a compelling business case. By compelling, we mean it contains all the information and analyses a decision maker needs for making well-informed decisions about a project. Each project has different drivers, opportunities, and challenges; therefore, each case will necessarily be different.

Module 2 helps Innovation Project Teams make sure they have selected the best business opportunity and that the organization does, indeed, have the ability to deliver the contemplated new product/service.

Subsystem 2A: Elaborate and Evaluate

Elaborate and Evaluate can be viewed as a second iteration of building an opportunity from an idea, as well as the preparatory step to developing the business case found in the second step of Module 2. Additional tools and assessments are provided to elaborate on the opportunity and ensure that as much value as possible is eventually realized from it.

Evaluation as meant here does not imply a decision to eliminate or continue a project, but rather to add value and create a prioritized list of opportunities for further development. By definition, all breakthrough ideas will incorporate challenges, so we encourage teams to take the necessary time, use the tools provided, and seek facts and data that transform ideas into strong and viable business plans.

Elaborate and Evaluate teaches users to research and select target markets, design differentiating strategies, and more fully define the market offering. It takes advantage of tools introduced in the TEC Algorithm, along with new techniques such as the Technology Readiness Level (TRL) assessment, to assist Innovation Project Teams in fully evaluating their idea for realistic business opportunities, as well as possible threats, through the analysis of market/product information. Among the tools are:

- CPM – Capability-to-Product-to-Market Elaboration Tree
- PAMM – Product Attribute and Market Matrix
- Buyer Utility Map

- Market and Technology Readiness
- S-Curve Analysis
- Intellectual Property Assessment
- Functional Assessments
- Strategic Assessments
- Value Proposition
- Opportunity Portfolio

Formal acceptance into the organization's innovation portfolio requires a documented business case. These tools will help you gather and organize the information necessary to inform your organization's decision makers.

Subsystem 2B: Develop Business Case

After the idea has been rendered as a real business opportunity and critical information has been gathered to compare it to other opportunities, the *Develop Business Case* step shows users exactly how to build a comprehensive and detailed business case. But rather than just focus on myriad financial proformas, the System requires the case to tell the story of why this innovation initiative is needed: What the solution is, what customer problem it solves, how it will be delivered, and how your solution is differentiated from those of competitors.

Teams must go back to the two conditions that qualified the opportunity in the first place and test their decision by considering the following questions:

1. Is there an enduring customer need?

- Is there a need or desire for our solution? Who wants it? Why?
- Does the solution take advantage of emerging long-term trends? (Political? Economic? Social? Technological?)
- Why are other people investing in this market?
- Is the size of the potential market adequate? Can it be expanded?

2. Do we possess the special capabilities needed to deliver the new product or service and win in the marketplace?

- Does our solution offer a competitive advantage?
- Do we have superior resources?

- Who can we partner with to deliver our solution?
- Does our brand permit us to address this market successfully?
- Can our competitive advantage be sustained?

Only after this story is clear and senior management is on board should Innovation Project Teams and their Sponsors concentrate on forecasting the financial results expected from the new opportunity.

Module 3: Adopt and Implement

How to implement the ideas they have developed presents a major challenge for most companies. New ideas can upset existing production and delivery capabilities, current sales and marketing practices, and existing supply chain partnerships, not to mention the financial model the firm uses to communicate with investors. Although most companies say they value innovation, implementation can be much more difficult, possibly requiring seismic changes in the organization's structure, culture, procedures, and even personnel.

Acquiring the resources necessary to fully develop and launch a new offering requires the cooperation and coordination of many people in many different disciplines and departments across the organization. The problem is, these people all have full workloads and tend to see anything new as trouble or, at a minimum, extra work.

That's why it takes a tremendous effort to get an innovation adopted in large organizations. Innovators mistakenly believe that if they come up with a good idea or a good opportunity, even a complete business case or plan, the organization will naturally adopt it. In reality, however, the organization is more likely to reject it.

Adoption often requires a new, integrated management system and new set of key performance indicators to guide the organization's innovation management program.

Subsystem 3A: Plan Adoption

Because of its importance, we will develop the process of adopting selected business cases in some detail. Given the difficulty and size of the issue, we provide six tools that help Innovation Project Teams prepare their concept for implementation by the organization.

These tools are a direct result of our experience with what it takes to introduce breakthrough opportunities into organizations that are stuck in incrementalism.

For example, the **Adoption Worksheet** makes sure that Sponsors, Gatekeepers, and other stakeholders are kept apprised and their input sought so there are no surprises as the project finishes development. Throughout the project, everyone whose participation and approval is essential must help innovation project teams traverse the Valley of Death without falling victim to the "not-invented-here" syndrome. A **Roles and Responsibilities Worksheet** identifies each person, or role, who should be involved in the project's development and delivery along with an expectation of his or her involvement across the project's entire discovery-development-delivery life.

In short, the System shines a powerful spotlight on this critical transition period.

Subsystem 3B: Govern and Measure

Govern and Measure is a unique subsystem. It introduces the new organizational structures and metrics needed to implement breakthrough innovation projects. It is applicable—and crucial—to the entire process.

Because the structure that supports emergent innovation is very different from a regular formal structure, different procedures are needed. A growing body of work shows how large organizations can use separate structures to support emergent and discontinuous innovation (1). The System incorporates this new knowledge and provides readers with tools to help create these structures.

We recommend that an Innovation Portfolio Committee preside over the organization's portfolio of investment projects. The Committee is a permanent, dedicated team. It is composed of the Innovation Leader and the key stakeholders (for example, Operations, Finance, Marketing, R&D, and Customer Support) needed to provide the management expertise essential to motivate personnel, evaluate projects, and allocate resources to breakthrough innovation opportunities.

The Committee must be a flexible team that can add members and scale to meet the unpredictable demands of innovation. It must have the authority to commission Innovation Project Teams to pursue specific opportunities. Most important, Committee members are accountable and evaluated on their performance outside of their official functions (2).

By contrast, Innovation Project Teams are temporary; they are assigned to a specific project that is to be completed within a designated budget and timeframe. Their to-do list might include, "investigate market opportunity X, prototype new solution Y with customer Z," and the like. The team will often include the idea Champion along with the people who possess the key technical skills required by the project (for example, Operations, Finance, Marketing, R&D, and Customer Support).

Innovation Project Teams are not only accountable to the business function they sit in, but to the Innovation Portfolio Committee as well.

Govern and Measure also provides users with a holistic approach to measuring their proficiency in managing breakthrough innovation as well as the strategic outcomes of their efforts.

But you can't manage what you don't measure. That's why *Govern and Measure* also provides users with a holistic approach to measuring both their proficiency in managing breakthrough innovation and the strategic outcomes of their efforts.

The System requires strong internal management practices such as Portfolio Management, Market Management, and Idea Management. (See Key Concepts below.) These practices are developed through iterative use of the System and application to numerous projects. Users are connected with a tool for measuring the progression, or maturation, of their innovation management practice: the CIMS Innovation Management Maturity Assessment (IMMA).

Govern and Measure explains how to develop strong, mature, innovation management capabilities that fit into an overall, balanced scorecard for managing your firm's business strategy. *Govern and Measure* is indeed a special subsystem; it makes breakthrough innovation a strategic imperative and part of the normal operations of the firm.

Key Concepts

In addition to the three-module process, the System embodies six key concepts:

- Doing the Right Projects
- Integrated Go-Kill Decisions
- Culture Eats Strategy for Breakfast
- Speed to Market

- Iteration and Skills-Building
- Big Data Analytics for Big Decisions

These concepts don't confine themselves to any one subsystem, or even a module, but rather pervade the entire System. Readers should think of these concepts as the foundation the System is built upon. The good news is that through repeated use of the System, the importance of these concepts will become clearer, as will the management tactics for leveraging them.

Doing the Right Projects

At its core, the CIMS System contains a detailed Idea Management process that describes all of the activities that must take place before an opportunity is adopted into the formal new product development (NPD) processes of the company. As discussed, these activities mirror the roles that Champions, Sponsors, and Gatekeepers perform in order to traverse the Valley of Death. And they are laid out in step-wise fashion so users know what needs to be done next in order to develop their ideas into business innovations.

However, to ensure that the best (right) opportunities are selected for implementation, readers must be aware of—and their organizations proficient in—two other innovation management competencies: Market Management and Portfolio Management. These two competencies act as the rudder and compass for guiding and selecting which ideas to develop and ultimately which opportunities to pursue.

Market Management

Market Management provides a market-understanding framework that allows the organization to focus on the pursuit of profitable markets, customers, and business opportunities. This framework relies on developing insight—through research and fact-based analysis of market data—that identifies and anticipates potential market opportunities consistent with the organization's strategic direction.

The long-term competitiveness of any company depends ultimately on the acceptance and attractiveness of its product and service offerings in the marketplace. A differentiated offering is critical for generating profits, improving market position, creating new standards, and developing new, niche markets.

Market information exists in many forms, however. Meaningful marketplace insight requires an understanding of market behavior, including the company's macro-environment, customers, and competition.

Portfolio Management

Portfolio Management is the dynamic decision process that articulates the organization's business strategy in terms of a set of development and operating investments. In this process, the appropriate mix of investment types is determined; new investments are evaluated, selected, and sequenced; and existing investments may be accelerated, killed, or reprioritized. The process is characterized by uncertain and changing information, dynamic opportunities, multiple goals and strategic considerations, interdependent investments, and multiple decision makers.

Although Portfolio Management is complex and challenging, it is also vital to ultimately attaining the firm's targeted business performance objectives. For many organizations, the management of R&D/technology investments focuses primarily on managing individual projects. Portfolio Management is often relegated to a once-a-year project prioritization event.

As a result, Portfolio Management, as typically practiced, is a misnomer. Effective Portfolio Management is much more than simply creating a list of prioritized projects for the annual budgeting exercise.

The symptoms of ineffective or weak Portfolio Management practices and their impact on the organization's top and bottom lines are significant. Without a Portfolio Management discipline, the end result is a scattershot effort that does not support the organization's strategic direction. In this case, the portfolio is unfocused; it contains too many projects and, hence, spreads resources too thinly. In addition, many of the projects are of marginal value, and the portfolio is poorly balanced.

To learn more about building strong capabilities in Portfolio Management and how it affects strategy, see the *Govern and Measure* section of Chapter 6, *Module 3: Adopt and Implement.*

The importance of Portfolio Management to the System cannot be overstated (3). As previously described, breakthrough innovations are often viewed as risky because they challenge the organization's current business model. Moreover, companies have many other priorities vying for their attention and resources. For companies that intend to adopt and implement the breakthrough innovations developed in Modules

1 and 2, they first have to make these innovations an official and well-communicated part of the organization's strategy and investment portfolio. A strong practice in Portfolio Management achieves this. Without it, breakthrough innovations—no matter how compelling—will be starved for resources. They'll wither and eventually die.

Integrated Go/Kill Decisions

A common problem we observe at many companies is that they seem incapable of stopping anything! While individual projects may have been passing their checkpoints, as a set they were not creating the overall portfolio value the organization needed to justify their continuation. Consequently, a two-tier project selection system is essential; without it, the organization's Portfolio Management capability is substantially weakened, with the result that marginal projects continue to consume valuable resources that by all rights should be surrendered to more promising, strategically aligned projects.

Management needs to make considered Go/Kill decisions whenever they allocate resources to a project (4). While it's essential that they make the tough calls at these checkpoints, managers need to be mindful of the impact their decisions have on the portfolio and vice versa. Project decisions need to harmonize with overall portfolio decisions in order to yield a balanced and aligned portfolio of high-value projects that directly support the company's overall business strategy.

Specifically, the Innovation Portfolio Committee and Innovation Project Teams must work together to identify poor/weak projects earlier. This gives the organization the ability to kill projects that no longer fit with the portfolio's objectives as soon as they are identified

All projects need to be brought under this control and discipline so that renegade projects do not sap the firm's resources and dilute the portfolio. It is imperative that management quickly reassigns its resources whenever a decision is made to kill a project. By not acting—or acting too slowly—on its decisions, senior management delays new opportunities and runs the risk of demoralizing the organization.

Culture Eats Strategy for Breakfast

The Innovation Portfolio Committee has another equally important job: to reshape and change culture. It does this by:

- Directing ideation. The Committee makes clear that the organization is not interested in just *any* idea, but in those that will advance the business.

- Ensuring transparency. The Committee will make sure everyone understands the idea submission and evaluation process. This transparency leads directly to building trust across and down through the organization, thereby building credibility for subsequent implementation.

- Assigning coaches to idea submitters. Coaches act as the conduit for formal communication with submitters and their supervisors about the funding decision; they help successful submitters develop their work plan and identify needed technical resources, while also providing encouragement and monitoring both project progress and budget.

- Giving idea submitters and their teams space. This involves providing Innovation Project Teams with the resources (human, capital, and so forth) to develop their idea as part of their regular jobs.

- Communicating successes to the rest of the organization.

A formally sanctioned mechanism like the Innovation Portfolio Committee, which funds and supports breakthrough innovation projects, is a cultural statement in itself and expands innovation prospects for employees at all levels.

Researchers have learned how organizational culture affects innovation structures. As long ago as 1983, Galbraith contended that innovative structures have roles, processes, and decision-making behaviors that are strikingly different from what he called operational structures (5).

Organizational structure associated with innovation is more likely quasi-formal and less constrained than operational structure, with its recursive learning loops and more interactions. Such a structure is based on an organizing principle of developing and maintaining long-term working relationships with various internal groups, as well as with external customers (6). An innovation culture that encourages individual learning and experimentation with new ideas contributes to successful innovation (7). For an organization to innovate, multiple organizational functions must learn and value the same things at the same time so that they can understand and cooperate with one another (8). As an organization learns new innovation routines, they create shared meanings across social and structural boundaries (9).

In short, creating such structures requires effort.

Multiple, formal ties must be created between the front-end processes of ideation and evaluation, including market intelligence and the creation of new business models for innovation, and the more operational structures that transition an idea into formal development.

Innovation Portfolio Committee members will likely have to acquire new leadership skills to help aspiring innovators demonstrate their potential and get their ideas accepted into the formal program. Innovators need to learn to express their ideas as business opportunities, rather than simply as technical advances.

Speed to Market

A chief objective of the System is to provide organizations with a process that enables the transition of breakthrough ideas across the Valley of Death to commercialization efficiently and effectively. For mature companies whose products or services risk commoditization and an inevitable revenue stall (see reference 1, chapter 1, *Introduction)* the speed of innovation decision-making and action to implementation is critical.

Organizations that can screen more ideas in less time will generate higher returns (10). Longitudinal benchmarking studies performed by the Product Development and Management Association over the past 20 years have shown that although companies are making great progress in reducing the total time to market, they are not reducing the time spent in the early phases of new product and service development (11).

This failure to speed up the early innovation phases might be attributed to the downsizing of critical discovery activities, like Voice of the Customer, Market and Competitive Intelligence, and so on. These are the activities and corporate functions that are dedicated to generating the data needed to make innovation decisions about new breakthrough products and services. For organizations focused solely on operational excellence, performing early-stage innovation activities fast is a distinct advantage.

Additionally, many mature firms are somewhat disconnected from their end users because they depend on third-party analysts for vital information about customer wants and needs, emerging technologies, the rising threat of new competitors, and more. Moreover, the problem is exacerbated by the sheer volume and variety of data that confronts companies today. Enough information is added to the Internet every day to fill 168 million DVDs. IBM has calculated that 90 percent of the world's data has been generated in just the last two years (12). How can organizations expect to extract valuable information from all of the noise in this tsunami of data? Even apparently relevant data collected and warehoused by the organization itself—such as customer satisfaction surveys, call center logs, and manufacturing process data—can be inaccessible. Its potential innovation content will remain a mystery to Innovation Project Teams who lack the proper tools for analyzing the information.

Our premise is that many mature firms lack the solid, well-grounded information needed to inform strategic decision-making. Consequently, they hesitate and defer making decisions. These firms also delay replacing current but endangered and obsolescing product and service platforms with new and competitive ones. Worse, the lack of good information makes all innovation look far more risky than simply continuing business as usual, which appears safe despite its strategic, existential risks.

Iteration and Skills-Building

Before actually starting work on a project, companies need to recognize the System's iterative nature. As you move from one worksheet to another in the following chapters, you may see some similarity in the topics. This is by design because opportunities do not develop in a linear fashion. Rather, original ideas must be revisited after information is gathered that changes the nature of the idea or the market space.

Project Work

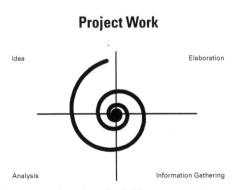

Figure 3-2. Project work progresses in an iterative fashion.

We see opportunities developing in an iterative fashion, as depicted in Fig. 3-2. An initial idea is generated and then elaborated upon. Information is gathered about the opportunity that should allow you to decide whether it will fill enduring customer needs and whether your company has the ability to deliver—including the willingness to change business models in order to capture the full value of the opportunity. This usually results in a change in one or more aspects of the project. Although initial iterations may result in large changes, over time the project stabilizes.

Another, equally important aspect of the System is that with each iteration—and with each successive project—companies learn more about how to develop breakthrough products and services. Practice, it seems, does make perfect.

Since the System is an iterative process that spans multiple functions, a broad range of expertise is needed to make progress. This expertise is often gathered by forming interdisciplinary teams. However, even teams can be slow, since every time a different topic is encountered a different person must be involved. Nevertheless, functional expertise does not ensure the ability to innovate. The process of innovation must be used to make innovation repeatable. Therefore, individuals must obtain the skills necessary to participate in innovation, which is truly an interdisciplinary activity.

In fact, a major objective of this handbook is to embed the skills of innovation in the reader.

Rather than depending on other people from disparate areas, we believe that each person should be capable of innovation. Like the TEC Algorithm before it, the System is light on process and heavy on developing the specific skills Innovation Project Teams need to define a breakthrough idea, build a viable and profitable business opportunity, and buttress their original concept with facts in order to develop a compelling business case.

The System does this through a series of self-defining, self-teaching templates, called worksheets. A few words about the worksheets:

- Ultimately each worksheet represents a section of the business case.
- Each worksheet asks Innovation Project Teams to consider only the critical information for that step in the process.

- Each worksheet builds on the preceding worksheet as Innovation Project Teams traverse the Valley of Death.
- All worksheets can and should be modified to fit the requirements of the project.

To help Innovation Project Teams find the information to populate the worksheets, the System provides a process for using Big Data analytics. Big Data analytics is an important information-gathering tool to facilitate breakthrough innovation. Innovation Project Teams do not need to hunt-and-peck on Google to piece together remnants of data gleaned from popular websites. Nor do they need to accompany their business case with a litany of assumptions when they lack the information they need to defend their positions. Now they can use sophisticated algorithms to gather and prioritize the information they need from high quality, vetted sources. This kind of power is transformative and, when added to the System, it empowers breakthrough innovation.

From our experience in testing the System in the classroom and on projects with companies, we see users quickly embracing its rubric. In fact, after having applied the worksheets once, we see users proceeding directly to the worksheets on subsequent projects. After only a short exposure to the System, users no longer need the handbook because they internalized the process. They only need to capture their decisions and supporting facts in the System's worksheets.

This bodes well for mature companies, which, as discussed, are almost totally reliant on third-party marketing intermediaries to research strategic questions. Now these companies can do this research—and breakthrough innovation—themselves.

Big Data Analytics for Big Decisions

As we have said, the System makes extensive use of Big Data analytics processes and technologies to help Innovation Project Teams expand their knowledge of what is knowable and discriminating for the big decisions they need to make about breakthrough initiatives. For the past five years, CIMS has been experimenting with natural language processing of unstructured text data—the kind of information that resides on the Internet in the form of websites, blogs, Wikis, research papers, government reports, conference papers, and presentations. Companies' customer satisfaction reports, call center logs, and other internal information is similarly stored as unstructured text data.

The goal of this handbook is to help companies sift through massive amounts of data that can help answer strategic questions. Retrieving such data—both internal and external to the company—used to be unaffordable, if not physically impossible. Easier access to information plus new analytical methods enables firms to ground their strategic decisions in timely, curated evidence.

As Innovation Project Teams progress through the System, they are confronted by a number of decision points: What exactly is the idea (*Define Idea*)? Does it represent a real business opportunity for the company (*Build Opportunity*)? And are there other alternative opportunities that show as much or more promise (*Elaborate and Evaluate*)?

These decision points act much like road signs at critical junctions. If teams lack sufficient knowable and discriminating information on which to base their decisions, they are instructed to go back and continue seeking facts to support them. The System supports that search.

To help teams gather and analyze the facts necessary to advance through these decision points, this handbook uses many of the venerable decision support tools for Big Data analytics: PESTEL, SWOT (13), VOC (14), and Market Segmentation.

With these tools, the System can now help teams answer questions such as:

- What are the major trends impacting our industry? (Political, Economic, Social, Technological, Environmental, and Legal—PESTEL Analysis)
- What are the best opportunities for our company? Do they leverage our strengths? What threats and weaknesses must we take into account? (Strengths, Weaknesses, Opportunities, Threats—SWOT Analysis)
- What are the expressed and unexpressed needs of customers in this market? (Voice of the Customer analysis)
- Which customer populations should we target? (Market Segmentation analysis)

You can learn more about the Big Data platform and process CIMS has created in Chapter 7, *Tools and Techniques*.

REFERENCES FOR CHAPTER 3

1. O'Connor, G.C. 2008. "Major Innovation as a Dynamic Capability: A Systems Approach." *Journal of Product Innovation Management*, 25: 313-330.

2. Markham, S. K., & Lee, H. 2013. "Use of an Innovation Board to Integrate the Front End of Innovation with Formal NDP Processes: A Longitudinal Study." *Research-Technology Management*, 56, 37-44.

3. Cooper, R.G., Edgett, S. J., and Kleinschmidt, E. J. 1999. "New Product Portfolio Management: Practices and Performance." *Journal of Product Innovation Management*, 16: 333-351.

4. Cooper, R.G. 1999. "The Invisible Success Factors in Product Innovation." *Journal of Product Innovation Management*, 16: 115-133.

5. Galbraith, J.R. 1983. "Designing the Innovating Organization." *Organizational Dynamics*, 10: 5-25.

6. Dougherty, D. 2001. "Reimagining the Differentiation and Integration of Work for Sustained Product Innovation." *Organization Science*, 12: 612-631.

7. McLean, L.D. 2005. "Organizational Culture's Influence on Creativity and Innovation: A Review of the Literature and Implications for Human Resource Development." *Advances in Developing Human Resources*, 7: 226-246.

8. Hardy, C., Lawrence, T.B., and Grant, D. 2005. "Discourse and Collaboration: The Role of Conversations and Collective Identity." *Academy of Management Review*, 30: 58-77.

9. Ulwick, A.W. 2005. *What Customers Want: Using Outcome-Driven Innovation to Create Breakthrough Products and Services*. McGraw-Hill, New York.

10. Markham, S.K. 2000. "Corporate Championing and Antagonism as Forms of Political Behavior: An R&D Perspective." *Organization Science*, 11: 429-447.

11. Markham, S.K., and Lee, H. 2013. "Product Development and Management Association's 2012 Comparative Performance Assessment Study." *Journal of Product Innovation Management*, 30: 408-429.

12. IBM. 2012. "Analytics: The Real-World Use of Big Data." Executive Report, IBM Institute for Business Value.

13. Panagiotou, G. 2003. "Bringing SWOT into Focus." *Business Strategy Review*, 14: 8-10.

14. Griffin, A., & Hauser, J. R. 1993. "The Voice of The Customer." *Marketing Science*, 12: 1-27.

Notes:

CHAPTER 4

Module 1: Convert Ideas into Opportunities

Ideas-Needs-Abilities

As introduced in Chapter 3, the System incorporates a process for turning ideas into innovations. Module 1 helps you define the idea by (1) establishing your intentions, (2) describing the idea in terms that are meaningful to management, and (3) substantiating the idea by clearly stating what is different and commercially promising. The second part of Module 1 builds the opportunity by (1) tying the idea to either an articulated or unarticulated need and (2) determining that the organization either has or can obtain the ability to deliver the new product/service/business concept embodied in that idea.

Define Idea

Activities in Module 1A: *Define the Idea* (see Fig. 4-1) are usually conducted informally in an ad hoc fashion by proponents, champions, sponsors, and other interested people such as users, customers, or suppliers. The proponents may be asked to engage in these activities, or they may be done by the individual on their own initiative.

System for Industrial Innovation

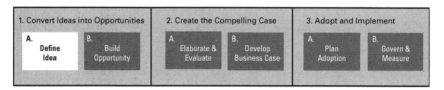

Figure 4-1. The CIMS System for Industrial Innovation begins by defining the product/service idea.

The idea, need, and ability are inseparably connected; when properly configured they form an opportunity. These relationships are depicted in Fig. 4-2 *Opportunity Development*. The terms in the figure are defined as follows:

- Idea: The recognition that something has commercial value.
- Need: An unmet desire on the part of a customer.
- Ability: Your company's ability to meet the customer need.
- Opportunity: An idea embedded in customer needs and your ability to deliver on the need.

As mentioned earlier, an idea is the recognition that something is likely to have commercial value. Ideas come in two ways. The first is through insights about customers: You recognize that your existing or potential customers need something. The other is through new or existing capability: You believe you either have or can obtain the ability to make or deliver something.

When you have a customer-need idea, you must substantiate that need in the market. Customer needs can either be articulated or unarticulated. Once you can specify a need, it is a straightforward step to state that need as an ability. The needs phrase "Customer X needs Y" becomes rephrased as, "We require the ability to deliver Y to customer X." This identifies the ability that can then be searched for.

Note that you do not have to possess the ability to meet a need at the time you become aware of the need.

For example, if customers want longer talk times for their cell phones, then one ability might be to make more powerful batteries. On the other hand, if you are a battery manufacturer developing a new, lighter, and more powerful battery using nano fibers, then you must state the ability to make this kind of battery as a customer need, in this case as a need for longer talk times for cell phones. We will review a number of ways to find new abilities, including the use of Big Data.

Stating either a need as an ability or an ability as a need can be challenging, and it is easy to get overwhelmed. The System provides the process and tools to guide you through this activity.

An idea can only become a real business opportunity when it is grounded in both enduring customer needs and your ability to deliver the product or service. You must state your idea as both a customer need and a new ability in order for the idea to be recognized as a valuable business opportunity.

Opportunity Development

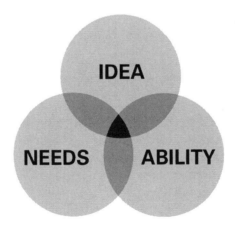

1. Idea + Ability = A product no one wants
2. Idea + Needs = A product you can't deliver
3. Needs + Ability = An unfocused product
4. Idea + Needs + Ability = Opportunity

Figure 4-2. Opportunity is confirmed when the need and ability to meet that need are verified.

At the end of this module, you will have defined the project; generated an initial idea; verified the idea in terms of articulated or unarticulated customer needs; rendered the needs as abilities; and found either an internal, external, or combination of solutions to fill those needs. This exercise may be conducted for multiple projects and compared, ranked, and prioritized by comparing opportunities in the **Portfolio Tool** at the end of this chapter.

Define the Idea

To define an idea you must:

1. specify the intended outcome,

2. describe the initial idea or concept that offers commercial benefit, and

3. substantiate the idea's value to a prospective customer.

For purposes of explanation, we define a product idea as anything of commercial value: You get paid for it. So we refer to both goods and services as product ideas. Ideas, however, are not products. At this early stage—before we understand the customer, market, or our ability to deliver anything to the market—ideas are simply the recognition that something could produce a benefit for the company, be it a good, service, business model, cost reduction, or competitive advantage.

Intended Outcome

Good ideas benefit your company in the marketplace, but too many ideas can also clog the decision-making process and waste resources. So before spending time brainstorming ideas that might prove irrelevant, you must determine the general parameters of the project, including objectives, time frame, and cost. Establishing the intended outcome requires making a number of preliminary decisions that define generally what you want to accomplish. The **Intention Worksheet** will help you organize your thoughts about that outcome. You do not need to answer all the questions. For example, if the purpose of the project is to explore a market space, you should not answer the technology question. In fact, you should be as focused as possible. The more radical your intention, the more questions you will answer. As with all the worksheets, you may need to add or modify some of the parts.

Intention Worksheet	
Question	**Answer**
What do you want to know?	
What market segments are you addressing?	
What needs do you want to explore?	
What technical area are you working to exploit?	
What new sources or solutions do you want to explore?	
What are you developing: a good or a service?	
What is the expected scope of the budget?	
What resources and infrastructure are required?	
What resources are available?	
What is the expected time frame?	
What is the expected size and cost of the project?	
What do you expect to return to the organization?	

Description of Initial Idea

Most likely, the initial idea is already apparent from answering the questions above. Skip to *Opportunity Development* if your idea is already chosen or at least well defined. Otherwise, after establishing your general intentions, you must formulate an initial idea description as a good or service product, business model, administrative change, cost reduction, partnership, merger or acquisition, or intellectual property.

The idea description consists of multiple parts; rather than only a simple physical description, it must include the intended target customers and how they could benefit. The **Idea Description Worksheet** will help you formulate or expand the initial idea description. You should have a response to all the items in this worksheet.

Idea Description Worksheet	
Item	**Description**
Physical description or service description	
Target users	
How will product be used?	
How does product benefit user?	
Commercialization path?	
Anticipated price?	

Idea Substantiation

High-potential ideas share three characteristics: (1) They are unique (no "me-too's" allowed!); (2) They promise an overt benefit or benefits; and (3) There is good reason to believe the idea can succeed in the marketplace. The following worksheets help you substantiate the value of your idea.

Unique Difference

The **Unique Difference Worksheet** lets you organize the ways in which the product idea differs from existing and/or competitive offerings or from ways your customers are already satisfying their needs. Add additional types of differences to match your project. Describe the difference in the "difference" column, and then indicate how strongly your idea differs from existing offerings.

Unique Difference Worksheet		
Type of Difference	**Difference**	**Strength of Difference**
Performance increase		
Cost reduction		
New capability		
Strategic advantage		

Overt Benefits

The **Overt Benefits Worksheet** states how the idea will clearly benefit your prospective customers. You should use a separate worksheet for each market segment.

Overt Benefits Worksheet		
Feature	**Benefit**	**Strength of Benefit**
Performance increase		
Cost reduction		
New capability		
Strategic advantage		

Reason to Believe

Most projects have one or more features that are critical to success. For example, a new technology might have promising performance characteristics, but there is doubt about the market need. Similarly, you might discover a strong need, but you have no feasible technology or you cannot obtain a license. In another scenario, there might be a demonstrable need and a clear solution, but the production cost would be too high. Whatever the project, you should assess the idea in terms of the skeptics' willingness to believe it can succeed.

Reason to Believe Worksheet		
	Reason to Believe	**Strength of Reason**
Success factor		
Technology		
Production capability		
Team time and fit		
Supply		
Distribution		
Competition		

Build Opportunity

After an idea is defined it must be turned into an opportunity (see Fig. 4-3). *Build Opportunity* has two parts. The first is to establish if and how the customer needs a product embodying your idea. This is done with the **Enduring Customer Needs Worksheet**. You will establish if the need is articulated or unarticulated and use a set of early-stage market research techniques to find each type of need. In particular, Big Data is very useful for finding unarticulated needs that may not be discovered any other way. We discuss that in Chapter 7, *Tools and Techniques*.

System for Industrial Innovation

1. Convert Ideas into Opportunities		2. Create the Compelling Case		3. Adopt and Implement	
A. Define Idea	B. Build Opportunity	A. Elaborate & Evaluate	B. Develop Business Case	A. Plan Adoption	B. Govern & Measure

Figure 4-3. After an idea is defined it must be turned into an opportunity.

Second, you must either have or be able to develop the needed capability to produce the product for it to be a real opportunity. Many companies have an extensive set of capabilities that are not evenly shared across the company. Too often, teams reinvent the wheel.

Activities in *Build Opportunity* are usually conducted by temporarily assigned teams in a defined fashion. The work necessary to develop the opportunity is significantly more involved than it was in the previous section. Therefore, it's up to the Innovation Leader to seek the support and participation of proponents and other people vital to the success of the team to ensure that process is completed in a timely and thorough manner.

Needs Search

Assuming the idea has been clearly stated, the next step is to identify the needs for that idea. It is not always clear what those needs are. What seems obvious from a distance becomes less clear up close when you are trying to decide which development path to take. That's why a rigorous, disciplined search process is important for both articulated and, especially, unarticulated needs.

The **Enduring Customer Needs Worksheet** is used to establish why customers need your idea and to determine whether or not there is a sufficient customer base for it.

Enduring Customer Needs Worksheet	
Describe the customers' need(s) for your intended solution.	
Can your customers articulate that need or not?	
Is there a demonstrable need or desire for your solution?	
Is the need consistent with long-term market or technology trends?	
Are other people investing in this market?	
Does the strength of the need and number of people with the need result in an acceptable potential market size?	

If the customer can articulate the needs for the idea, then a specific set of techniques can be used to capture those needs. However, customers may not be able to articulate their needs for more innovative, breakthrough ideas. In such cases, a different set of tools is used for understanding unarticulated needs.

Every search technique should include the following actions:

- Define and agree upon the objective.
- Set and agree on a time limit for the activity.
- Identify explicitly the time to categorize, condense, combine, and refine.
- Prioritize, rank, or list the appropriate development options.
- Capture and transfer the output of the inquiry to a master "hopper" spreadsheet or database for further refinement.
- Agree with other participants in the project on any actions and timescale following the meeting.
- Put a mechanism in place to control and monitor follow-up.

Articulated Needs Search

Many techniques are available to facilitate the expression of articulated needs. Although these techniques may seem obvious, the results are greatly improved when the proper techniques are selected and used in a disciplined way. The following techniques capture the needs the customer/user can articulate, from the simplest and least invasive to the most difficult and demanding techniques.

A more in-depth description of the techniques is found in Chapter 7: *Tools and Techniques.*

- **Direct Inquiry:** Interview knowledgeable respondents. Proper techniques increase the effectiveness of interviews.

- **Delphi Technique:** Send a question(s) to a set of experts who answer the questions independently. Send around everyone's answers and ask for comments. Repeat until no new information is gathered.

- **Nominal Group Technique:** A moderator poses a question to the group. Each member answers the question, which other members cannot discuss but only ask for clarification. Repeat the question until positions converge or separate positions become clear. This is the most effective way we know for finding creative solutions to problems. Proper technique is important for quality results.

- **Group Discussion:** Convene a group to discuss a specific issue. Proper use of roles, agendas, and methods will greatly improve effectiveness.

- **Discussion Prompts:** Present a prompt to a group as a way to think differently about a topic. For example, ask how the problem would be solved by a different group of people, by people in the past or future, or even how to make the problem worse.

- **Brainstorming:** A structured process to generate multiple approaches to an issue. Ideas are captured before assessment begins.

Unarticulated Needs Search

Unarticulated needs are those that users cannot state or do not yet know they have. They may be unaware of the need because they have a set way of doing things, they cannot conceive of a solution, or they simply do not know whether a new innovation can improve their work. The following techniques for finding unarticulated needs are ordered so that similar methods are close to each other. A more complete discussion of these techniques is found in Chapter 7, *Tools and Techniques.*

- **Elaboration:** Existing internal and external abilities are presented to intended users to see if they can recognize a use for them. Recognized uses may reveal unmet needs.

- **Strategy/Portfolio Review:** A structured process where unarticulated needs are identified by examining the existing set of ideas and possible blank spaces in the project portfolio. Blank portfolio spaces may reveal unmet needs that neither the developer nor users currently recognize.

- **Document or Library Search:** A process that identifies and systematically searches for internal and external documents related to the technology strategy. Comparing company activities with available solutions, emerging technologies, or practices at other companies can identify both needs and ideas. Needs being addressed by other companies may reveal unmet needs.

- **Early-Stage User Review:** A set of techniques to directly observe a cross section of users of established solutions that may reveal opportunities for improvements.

- **Voice of the Customer:** A structured process for interviewing potential users for ideas they may not have been able to articulate (1, 2).

- **Lead-User Research:** Engage your lead or most advanced users to understand how they use your existing solutions to identify and solve problems (3).

- **Technology Scouting:** Assesses the capabilities of new technologies in order to gain insight into which needs the new technologies are addressing.

- **PESTEL Analysis:** Assesses trends to identify capabilities the company must develop to compete in the future. These include Political, Economic, Social, Technological, Environmental, and Legal.

- **Environmental Scanning:** Examines the macro-environment, including PESTEL. Identifies opportunities the company may have nascent capabilities in.

- **Open Innovation:** A set of techniques to connect internal needs to external capabilities. Can also be used to assess which needs are being addressed externally. This can then be used to identify needs inside the company that are not being met (4).

These techniques and activities also yield the critical information needed to make sound innovation decisions. Big Data analytics can be a powerful aid to this process. It can greatly facilitate your ability to meet articulated or unarticulated needs, as well as to find internal or external sources of those abilities. For example, Natural Language Processing programs can analyze documents for critical information related to your search.

In addition, the ability to search unstructured text from any source can be used to locate and analyze extremely large numbers of documents related to your search. Chapter 7, *Tools and Techniques* provides a step-by-step process for using Big Data to search for needs and sources of capabilities.

Early-Stage Market Research

Identifying needs is the first step in confirming you have a real business opportunity. Early-stage market research has two main parts: customer needs identification and product validation. People sometimes rush to demonstrate that customers need their product as soon as they have the idea. Such validation work is premature when the market segments are not yet defined.

Customer Needs Identification includes three techniques to identify customer needs at an early stage: (1) Self as Customer, (2) Critical Observation, and (3) Voice of the Customer (VOC). These should be used at this stage for any new product, especially for the more radical ideas that we have been emphasizing. VOC is explained in Chapter 7, *Tools and Techniques.*

Product Validation involves establishing the adoption rate of the new product and is addressed in the "Rule of 4s and 5s," found in the Develop the Business Case section of Chapter 5, *Module 2: Create the Compelling Case.*

Ability Search

In addition to identifying customer needs, you may also need to search for the ability to deliver on those needs. See Chapter 7 for more details. Companies often have abilities they fail to profit from because they either do not understand or know of a customer need or internal use for them. For example, many companies have technologies that were patented but never commercialized. Similarly, they may have embedded skills or resources that could be of value to their customers if only they understood their customers' needs.

After the different needs for an idea are established, each need is translated into an ability to deliver. That ability may be a new product or service, an enhancement to an existing offering, or even a technology that has not yet been developed. Turning needs into abilities to deliver is applicable to both articulated and unarticulated needs.

As previously discussed, just as a need can be restated as an ability, so can abilities be restated as needs. An example of how this can be expressed is, "We have Ability X that meets Need Y." In fact, a given ability may meet many customer needs in various markets. The question is, who needs Y? In the past, this has been a very difficult question to answer. It required teams of technical and marketing analysts poring for months over hundreds of documents to arrive at a tentative, often risky, solution.

Questions surrounding needs can often be answered comprehensively using Big Data. The 8-Step process described in Chapter 7, *Tools and Techniques* has the power to leverage a team of technical and marketing experts to search through tens of millions of documents from a variety of sources in over 20 languages. This automated process cannot be duplicated by any other means. It provides a core capability of the System. For one thing, it enables companies to quickly and easily discover what's being said on social media, a platform that can provide vast amounts of information revealing specific customer needs. Similarly, Big Data analytical techniques also allow searching company, university, government, and public databases for market information, as well as sources of solutions to deliver on the needs.

The **Ability to Deliver Worksheet** will help you assess whether your company has the specialized capabilities required to deliver on that need or whether you need to conduct an external search for a solution.

Ability to Deliver Worksheet	
Will our solution have competitive advantage?	
Do we have superior technology and other resources?	
Who can we partner with to deliver solutions?	
Does our brand permit us to address this market?	
Can our competitive advantage be sustained?	

Searching for a solution is different from searching for a need. Searching for needs focuses on the potential users of any new product, service, or knowledge. Searching for abilities, in contrast, focuses on potential sources of capabilities rather than on users. These capabilities could take the form of a business model, service, product expansion, or new technology. Any of these abilities may reside internally or externally or within a long-term R&D project.

Internal Ability Search

Like the search for articulated needs, these techniques for searching internally range from the simplest and least invasive to the most difficult and demanding. (See Chapter 7 for more details.) They include:

- **Interview Experts**: Identify experts to interview for ideas that could meet needs. Adopting the interviewing techniques professionals use will greatly increase your effectiveness.

- **Consult on Needs with Communities of Practice or Other Networks**: Assemble a formal or informal network and either solicit their ideas for meeting the need yourself or ask a member to do so.

- **Document or Library Search**: Systematically search for internal and external documents related to technology solutions. Big Data techniques are well suited for this.

- **Convene a Workshop**: Adapt group-meeting techniques described in Chapter 7, *Tools and Techniques* to focus on finding ideas for a solution that meets the need rather than finding a need itself.

External Ability Search

Use these techniques to search for ability *outside* the company. See Chapter 7 for an in-depth discussion.

- **Query External Archival Sources**: Conduct typical literature search for solutions to meet needs.

- **Big Data/Natural Language Analytics**: Explore the many formal and informal information sources to identify emerging capabilities and solutions in different disciplines and industries.

- **Attend Conferences and Meetings**: Identify the best conferences in your area and arrange meetings with speakers, conference organizers, and attendees ahead of and after the meeting. Write an after-action report and share with internal constituents.

- **Consult Outside Associations or Consortia**: Present your needs to a relevant outside organization.

- **Seek out Consultants, Vendors, Universities, National Labs, or Other Experts**: Contact outside information specialists for assistance in developing search criteria and options for decision-making.

- **Technology Roadmapping**: Use this methodology to forecast future technical capabilities along different technology development paths.

- **Competitor Analysis**: Gather information about competitor actions, including investments, product offerings, vendor relationships, supply chain actions, patents, trademarks, copyrights, publications, presentations, and financial analysis.

- **Market Intelligence**: Obtain information about the market space the company is selling products into, including competitors, customers, regulatory agencies, consumer groups, advocacy groups, and other stakeholders.

The **Opportunity Development Worksheet** is an iteration on the Needs and Ability Searches. Here you will restate the results of your searches in two steps: Translate your idea into a customer need, and show how the organization has the ability to meet that need (which means it presents a real business opportunity). When you have grounded the idea in enduring customer needs and the ability to deliver, you have created that opportunity.

Opportunity Development Worksheet	
State your idea:	
Needs	
What customer insight(s) suggests there is commercial value?	
What new or existing abilities suggest there is commercial value?	
State your idea in terms of what needs it addresses.	
Can the customers articulate their need?	

Opportunity Development Worksheet	
What must be done to find unarticulated needs?	
Your organization's abilities	
State the ability that would be required to meet the need.	
Suggest new abilities that would meet a need.	
What must you do to find the ability?	
Opportunity statement	
Describe how the idea is grounded in an enduring customer need.	
Describe your existing or new ability to deliver on the need.	

Value Proposition

With the opportunity clearly stated, you are ready to write a value proposition for it. From the information gathered thus far in *Module 1: Convert Ideas into Opportunities,* use the **Value Proposition Worksheet** to write a short, precise value proposition (three sentences are optimum). It will also be used in the Opportunity Portfolio (below) and will be revised at the end of Chapter 5, *Module 2: Create the Compelling Case* after additional information is gathered and analyses are completed.

The value proposition is the foundation of the business model described in the second half of Chapter 5, *Module 2: Create the Compelling Case;* it's used in the business case executive summary and as the elevator pitch to succinctly communicate the value of your project to your senior managers and other interested parties.

The first sentence identifies the target customers by naming them and their needs. It also names the solution or offering you are making and states the need and benefit the customers derive from your offering. The customers here could be any internal or external users, buyers, recipients, stakeholders, or partners affected.

The second sentence compares your offering with existing methods to meet the need and states why you are different. Finally, in the third sentence, you make a direct statement about what you want the intended audience to do—such as invest, buy the product, or support further development.

Value Proposition Worksheet	
Structure	**Information**
First sentence	
For (target customer)	
Who (statement of the need or opportunity)	
The (product or service name)	
That (statement of benefit)	
Second sentence	
Unlike (primary competitive offering)	
Our offering (statement of primary differentiation)	
Third sentence	
Therefore, we request (list specifics)	

Opportunity Portfolio

Now that the project idea has been carefully defined as having an enduring customer need and your organization has the ability to meet it, you have a potential business opportunity. Nevertheless, just because an idea is turned into an opportunity does not mean the company should develop it. There may be better opportunities or other strategic reasons to pursue one opportunity over another.

The opportunity portfolio is created in three steps: (1) Restate the opportunity in terms of needs and abilities in the **Opportunity Description Worksheet**; (2) Numerically rate each project on the dimensions of needs and ability on the **Portfolio Score Worksheet**; and (3) Plot the opportunities on the **Portfolio Assessment Worksheet**.

The **Opportunity Description Worksheet** is another iteration that will help you state the potential of all opportunities in preparation for using the *Portfolio Tool* to compare the different opportunities fairly, by using similar terms. This worksheet helps to state all opportunities in a common language preparatory to using the *Portfolio Tool*.

Opportunity Description Worksheet	
Describe the idea	
What is its commercial value?	
What customers does it serve?	
How do those customers benefit?	
What are the articulated and unarticulated needs your idea satisfies?	
How will the company deliver the product to market profitably?	
What is its unique advantage?	
What critical elements make this likely to succeed?	

After all the opportunities have been described, use the **Portfolio Score Worksheet** to compare the different ideas using the same language and business criteria. Most often, needs will be identified that require a solution, and sometimes abilities will be identified that must be matched to a need.

Construct a spreadsheet with two principal parts: Customer Need and Ability to Deliver. Use the **Portfolio Score Worksheet** as a template to rate each opportunity on those dimensions. You will need to develop your own rating according to the nature of the opportunity. For example, you could rate each need item from 1-5 and take an average.

Portfolio Score Worksheet			
Customer Need	1=Low 5=High	**Ability to Deliver**	1=Low 5=High
Describe the need being filled		Describe how the product will be delivered	
Clarity of need		In-house development capability	
Strength of need		Known external capabilities	
Size of market		Potential for additional production increase	
Immediacy of need		Subject matter experts	
Durability of need		Technical viability	

Portfolio Score Worksheet			
Ease of market research		Quality system available to ensure product acceptability	
Sales cycle		Reasonable ability to deliver on time	
Trial		Acceptable project cost	
	Average		Average

After the opportunities are rated and averaged in terms of customer need and ability to deliver, plot them on the **Portfolio Assessment Worksheet**. Begin by plotting the average of needs and abilities on the Assessment. You can enrich the portfolio analysis by representing each opportunity as a circle whose area is the size of the opportunity. The circles could be colored to represent how important the idea is to the company or any other variable.

Portfolio Assessment Worksheet

Area = size of the opportunity   Color = importance

For example, in the following figure (Fig. 4-4), opportunity No. 2 is a large and important opportunity that meets a customer need better than opportunity No. 1, and the company is also better able to deliver No. 2. In contrast, opportunity No. 3 both meets the customer need better and the company has a stronger ability to deliver; unfortunately, it is a small opportunity.

Portfolio Assessment Example

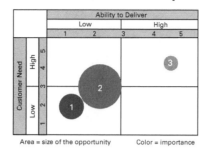

Figure 4-4. Portfolio Assessment for Opportunity No. 1.

In this simple example, opportunity No. 1 would not be pursued any further. Not only are customer needs determined to be "low," but the organization's ability to deliver a product or service that would satisfy these needs is also very "low." The organization would need to undergo a considerable amount of change to its business model for a questionable return.

Conversely, opportunity No. 3 might be pursued. The customer needs for this opportunity are "high" as are the organization's ability to deliver such a solution. Further work could expand the market space for this opportunity.

Less obvious is what to do with opportunity No. 2. The size of the market is bigger than both opportunities 1 and 3, yet customer needs are determined to be only average. Also, the organization's ability to deliver a viable solution is judged to be "low."

Recommended Actions:

- The decision team should see if it could gather more information about the customer needs for opportunity No. 3. Specifically, additional market mapping may identify "stronger, clearer, immediate, and more durable" needs associated with a segment of customers that represent a smaller but better opportunity for the organization.

- At the same time, the team should explore partnering with companies outside the organization in order to acquire the external capabilities needed to deliver the solution. Changing the organization's business model for this opportunity may be justified.

As a general rule, subsequent iterations on an opportunity should attempt to find information that would move it up and to the right, thereby reducing its market and technical risk to the organization.

At this point, you should have defined the project, generated an initial idea, verified the idea in terms of articulated or unarticulated customer needs, rendered the needs as abilities, and found either an internal, external, or combination of solutions to fill those needs. This exercise may be conducted for multiple projects and compared, ranked, and prioritized by comparing opportunities in the **Portfolio Assessment Worksheet**.

With all the ideas and chosen dimensions of evaluation displayed, your decision team is now in a position to decide which projects should be elaborated upon and subjected to further evaluation, and the compelling business case prepared.

REFERENCES FOR CHAPTER 4

1. Katz, G.M. 2001. "The 'One Right Way' to Gather the Voice of the Customer." *PDMA Visions Magazine*, 25: 1-6.

2. Markham, S.K. 2007. "Methods for Conducting Early Market Research." *Entrepreneurship.org*, the online publication of the Kauffman Foundation. Accessed July 2014. http://www.entrepreneurship.org/resource-center/methods-for-conducting-early-market-research.aspx

3. Von Hippel, E. 1986. "Lead Users: A Source of Novel Product Concepts." *Management Science*, 32: 791-805.

4. Chesbrough, H.W. 2003. *Open Innovation: The New Imperative for Creating and Profiting from Technology*. Harvard Business Press, Cambridge, Massachusetts.

Notes:

CHAPTER 5

Module 2: Create the Compelling Case

What's Critical

The challenge in writing a compelling business case is to understand what is critical and provide in-depth analysis for those items. At the same time, it's important to recognize the less important issues and not overwhelm the decision maker with information and analysis that does not improve the quality of the decision. While a complete plan will at some point be necessary, the decision to continue or ramp up a project must focus on the critical elements of success for that specific project. Decision makers will often reject an idea if the critical information is not separated from the mundane.

Activities in *Elaborate and Evaluate* should be conducted by permanently assigned teams in a managed way. The work necessary to develop the opportunity is much more extensive than the previous section. Therefore, proponents and other necessary people must be assigned by the Innovation Leaders and their supervisors to engage in these activities. You will prepare for writing your business case by using the series of in-depth tools in this chapter to elaborate on the opportunity developed in Chapter 4, *Module 1: Convert Ideas into Opportunities.* Later in this chapter, in the **Value Proposition Worksheet,** the value proposition is restated and plotted again.

Elaborate and Evaluate

System for Industrial Innovation

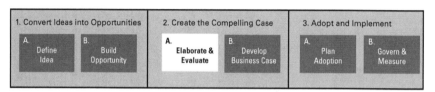

Figure 5-1. An opportunity must be elaborated on and evaluated before a compelling business case can be formulated.

An opportunity must be elaborated upon and evaluated before the business case is written. As we noted, this step can be seen as a second iteration of building an opportunity from an idea, as well as the preparatory step to writing a compelling business case.

At this point, the opportunity has been connected to a customer need, and the company has confirmed its ability to deliver on that need. Module 2 provides the tools to elaborate or expand on and evaluate the value of the idea. As opportunities are evaluated, ways to enhance the value are found. For example, additional market segments might be identified, additional product features might be added, and fondly-held attributes might be eliminated. Similarly, additional evaluation tools will be used to ensure that all facets of the opportunity are assessed for fatal flaws and all assumptions are verified.

In this way, elaborate and evaluate go together. We stress, again, that evaluation in this sense does not imply a decision to terminate or continue a project but rather to find and exploit facets of the opportunities.

Using the *Opportunity Portfolio Tool*, the team decides which project(s) will have a business case developed. Each opportunity should be subjected to one or more of the evaluative tools listed below. Not every tool must be used with every opportunity, but the list is ordered to increase the value of an opportunity.

1. CPM – Capability-to-Product-to-Market Elaboration Tree

2. PAMM – Product Attribute and Market Matrix

3. Buyer Utility Map

4. Market and Technology Readiness

5. S-Curve Analysis

6. Intellectual Asset Plan

7. Functional Assessment

8. Strategic Assessment

9. Value Proposition II

10. Portfolio Assessment

The first three tools—*CPM, PAMM,* and *Buyer Utility Map*—elaborate on how the product idea is embedded in enduring customer needs. The *CPM* matches the intended product with the right customers by developing multiple product manifestations of the capability and then matching those product ideas with customer segment needs. The *PAMM* then helps you choose which segment to enter by assessing the strength of the segment for each product attribute. Finally, the *Buyer Utility Map* increases your understanding of how the buyer will benefit from your product.

The next three tools elaborate on the ability represented by the new opportunity to deliver on the need. The *Readiness Scales* identify level of development and the requisite next development steps. The *S-Curve Analysis* elaborates on the difference between your new offering and existing offerings.

The *Intellectual Asset Plan* delves into your ability and willingness to protect the uniqueness of your opportunity.

The *Functional* and *Strategic Assessments* evaluate the opportunity in greater detail. These assessments help identify any fatal flaws and build the logic of the opportunity to include all the various parts needed to evaluate it rigorously.

The *Value Proposition II* is an informed reiteration of the previous *Value Proposition* in Chapter 4, *Module 1: Convert Ideas into Opportunities*. That proposition was a hypothesis to be tested; the second *Value Proposition* should be a defensible opportunity. In this version, the terms should be specific and verifiable. For example, at this point you should have specific information about your customer needs. Finally, you will use *Opportunity Portfolio II*, to decide which opportunity to write a business case for.

Capability-Product-Market (CPM)

An idea embraces specific capabilities that, in turn, are rendered as product features. A set of product features aimed at a specific customer comprises a product. The customer represents a target market. A single capability can lead to multiple products. Similarly, a single product may appeal to multiple markets.

This technique turns a single capability into multiple products, links each product to multiple potential market segments, and elaborates upon the original capability until sufficient value becomes evident. In this way, CPM allows you to systematically explore and answer the question management so often asks: What other avenues have you examined?

The **Capability-Product-Market (CPM) Linkage Worksheet** provides a space for describing the idea and what makes it unique. The idea is then elaborated upon by brainstorming product/service/business model options to generate multiple product manifestations of the idea. For example, an algorithm to decompose speech patterns could be a stand-alone piece of software, a web-based application, an add-on to an existing program, or even a software developer's kit. Finally, each product idea is linked to a market need. It is possible to use the CPM concept in reverse, using market needs to define products. However, this approach often creates more incremental options.

Capability-Product-Market Linkage Worksheet		
Capability	**Product Manifestations**	**Market Segments**
Description (Uniqueness) (Capabilities)	Product 1	Market 1 (needs)
		Market 2 (needs)
		Market 3 (needs)
	Product 2	Market 4 (needs)
		Market 5 (needs)
		Market 6 (needs)
	Product 3	Market 7 (needs)
		Market 8 (needs)

Product Attribute and Market Matrix (PAMM)

Not all market segments are equally attractive, nor might all possible segments be identified in the CPM tool. The **PAMM Worksheet** helps to elaborate on attractive segments. The features and attributes of all the Ps, or products, from the CPM are listed in the left-hand column of the PAMM, and all the potential markets are entered as column headings. Additional segments are identified as they become evident. For example, a power semiconductor may find immediate use in laptop computers but, later, in tablets, smart phones, and other hand-held electronic devices, which are also identified. In this way, the market opportunity is elaborated upon.

PAMM: Product Attribute and Market Matrix Worksheet						
	Market A		**Market B**		**Market C**	
	Seg 1	Seg 2	Seg 1	Seg 2	Seg 1	Seg 2
Attribute 1						
Attribute 2						
Attribute 3						
Attribute 4						
Attribute 5						

The cells in the **PAMM Worksheet** identify which product features or attributes are most attractive to which market segments. Depending on the product feature and possible segment response, you might enter a Yes or No in the cell; a number from 1 to 5; or High, Medium, or Low. You should decide on the scale to use, but be aware that different attributes may have different scales. For example, one attribute might be regulatory acceptance, which could be evaluated as Yes or No; or it could be a High, Medium or Low cost; or a very specific attribute like size or weight.

What you are looking for is where to position the product to enter and expand in the market. You are trying to identify those attributes that are most important to particular segments. At the same time, you can position the new product idea against competing products and market needs. The PAMM helps to elaborate on features and markets and derive additional uses for the product. Most important, it helps you understand the value added to each market segment.

Buyer Utility Map

The **Buyer Utility Map Worksheet** takes the PAMM one step further to show how a customer could benefit from your product. A separate Map is constructed for each cell in the PAMM; naturally, only complete **Buyer Utility Maps** for the most promising cells. After you determine the relationship between a product feature and a segment, the Map helps to articulate exactly how the customer benefits from the intended product. The different ways buyers might derive benefit are listed in the left column while stages of ownership are across the top. The benefit derived by the buyer is entered into each cell. Not every cell will have a benefit. In fact, it is often the case that a single cell justifies the project. Additional uses of the product can also be identified with the **Buyer Utility Map.**

For a particular product idea (not just the general opportunity), you identify and modify the stages of ownership and customer benefits. Each cell is then evaluated on a scale from 1 (low) to 9 (high) for how much utility or benefit a customer derives in that cell. For example, if a product is easy to buy, the first cell under "Buy Product" might be rated High if the intended customer segment highly values ease of purchase. Most cells will likely be rated 1 or left blank. The purpose is to substantiate your understanding of how the intended customers benefit and value your product.

Buyer Utility Map Worksheet						
Features	Find Product	Buy Product	Use Product	Share Product	Maintain Product	Dispose of Product
Easy to do						
Convenient						
Prestige						
Economical						
Reliable						
Quality						

Market and Technology Readiness

In preparing a business case, it is critical to describe the opportunity in terms of how much more work needs to be done. The **Market and Technology Readiness Worksheet** is patterned after NASA's famous Technology Readiness Level (TRL), which was used to determine how close a new idea was toward being able to fly. We have added a corresponding Market Readiness Level (MRL) to help determine the commercial readiness of the opportunity.

For the purposes of long-term research, only TRL 0-2 opportunities are considered. Opportunities that are judged as TRL 3-7 would be considered part of traditional R&D and directed appropriately (1). How you use the readiness level will depend on your project's intentions, goals, and resources. With both the TRL and MRL, simply pick the number that corresponds to the level of readiness and record it at the bottom of the worksheet.

Market and Technology Readiness Worksheet			
Level	Technology	Level	Market
1	Basic principles observed and reported	1	Basic market need observed
2	Technology concept and/or application formulated	2	Market needs for a specific target market articulated
3	Analytical and experimental critical function and/or characteristic proof of concept	3	Market needs validated through preliminary demonstration

Market and Technology Readiness Worksheet			
4	Component and/or breadboard validation in laboratory environment	4	Product attributes and features established
5	Component and/or breadboard validation in relevant environment	5	Other product dimensions of price, place, promotion established
6	System/subsystem model or prototype demonstration in a relevant environment	6	Product concept tested in intended market. Market size verified
7	System prototype demonstration in an operational environment	7	Product acceptance demonstrated in market trial
8	Actual system completed and qualified through test and demonstration	8	Product feature validated in test market
9	Actual system proven through successful operations	9	Product in market with proven sales
_____	Technology Readiness Score (Rate your technology according to the 1 to 9 scale)	_____	Market Readiness Score (Rate your opportunity according to the 1 to 9 scale)

S-Curve Analysis

The *S-Curve Analysis* takes the *Market and Technology Readiness* concept further by plotting the time and effort to develop a product opportunity against its performance. Generally speaking, this follows an "S" curve (see Fig. 5-2). It usually takes some time and effort until the product starts to perform. Improvements then quickly add to how well it performs. However, a given opportunity has limits on its performance; beyond a certain point, performance tapers off even if more effort is expended.

The *S-Curve* can be used to plot how effort leads to performance for multiple ideas. When this is done for competing opportunities, both inside and outside the company, it reveals the competitive potential of the new opportunity over time. This helps companies decide how to develop an opportunity to maximize its potential and compete most effectively against rivals.

To use the *S-Curve*, plot the performance for your competing ideas over time and plot how your underlying capability performs compared to the competition. Be sure you are comparing equivalent performance dimensions.

You may need to produce multiple charts in order to explain the competitive advantage of your opportunity compared to other ideas over time.

S-Curve Analysis

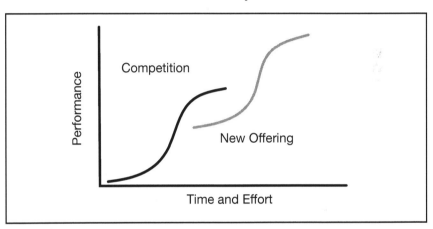

Figure 5-2. An S-Curve Analysis reveals how time and effort may lead to performance.

Intellectual Asset Plan

Once you become aware that your proposed product might provide a competitive advantage, the **Intellectual Asset Plan Worksheet** can help you assess the need for intellectual property protection. It also helps define the status of the IP, the strategic use for it, and the steps that need to be taken as part of your business plan.

Intellectual Asset Plan Worksheet

Name of Project Leader:			Date:	
Project Title/R&D Program:				
Brief Project Description:				

Technology Readiness Level?	(✓)	Has this idea been disclosed? When?	

Type of Intellectual Asset. What is unique (novel) about the idea?	License	Is there an IA strategy in place? Who is responsible for IA management?	
	Invention		
	Algorithm		
	Workflow		
	Method		(✓)

How will the IP be protected?	Patent	Where will the IP be protected?	US Only	
	Trade Secret		PCT	
	Copyright		Non-PCT	
	Other		All	

Has competitor due diligence and freedom to operate review been carried out on the IP?		Are third parties involved in development of IP? Who? Why?	
Is the technology commercialization strategy in place?		Are there agreements in place to manage confidentiality, background & foreground IP?	

70

Intellectual Asset Plan Worksheet			
What is the company's proposed stake/commer-cialization strategy in the IP?	Exclusive ownership		Licensing/Cross licensing?	
	Joint ownership			
	Exclusive license			
	Non-exclusive license		Field(s) of use required	
	Public disclosure			
	Other			
What is the value of the IP? What business leverage do we get?			Communication Plan. What types of publications are planned?	
Who will use the IP? What will the adopting unit use the IP for? How familiar is the adopting unit with the idea?			Are there plans for deployment in other assets/rest of industry? What is the roadmap for the technology in the next 5 yrs.? 10 yrs. and beyond?	

Functional Assessment

Opportunities must succeed on all dimensions, not just needs and abilities. A *Functional Assessment* looks at the opportunity from the perspective of all the relevant business functions. This interdisciplinary view helps to review and refine the product concept, force an awareness of the issues created in all functions, and verify information and assumptions. The functions include Legal, Market, Technology, Organization, Operations, and Finance (see Fig. 5-3). The objectives are to examine the opportunity for fatal flaws, test assumptions, and understand the value of the idea.

A *Functional Assessment* is conducted for each product concept. The assessment may need to be revised if information discovered in one functional area impacts the product concept. *Functional Assessments* are also the mechanism for collecting information necessary to conduct the *Strategic Assessments* in the next section.

As shown in Fig. 5-3, when a product idea enters into the *Functional Assessment*, it is assessed on the six functional areas. At any time a decision can be made to: (1) move the project forward, (2) stop working on the project and transfer it to a database, or (3) redefine the product concept based on information that becomes available in the functional assessment. It is important to recognize that this process may go through a number of iterations as more information leads to a redefinition of the product. It is important to start the *Functional Assessment* with a solid product concept. Too often, teams that struggle with the assessments do not understand each other's thoughts about the product.

Functional Assessments provide an integrated and cross-disciplinary perspective that is vital to innovation

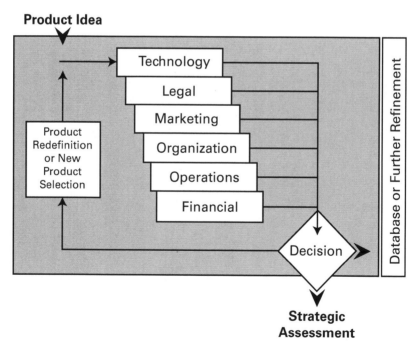

Figure 5-3. Functional Assessment ties the opportunity to its relevant organizational functions.

The **Functional Assessments Worksheet** is complex, so we first define the various parts of the worksheet and then explain how to use it:

- The first column of numbers on the far left contains the question numbers for each functional area.
- The second column is the importance of each assessment criteria.
- The third column is the actual assessment criteria.
- The fourth column is the rating of the criteria. The criteria are anchored on the left by terms that represent a low or disadvantageous score. On the right are terms that represent a positive score. Low scores are always "1," and high scores are always "5."
- The SWOT column is used to identify the assessment criteria that represent a Strength, Weakness, Opportunity, or Threat. You will use these items later in the *SWOT Analysis*.
- The questions are divided into the six functional areas.
- Each set of functional area questions is further divided into "Potential" questions that assess how valuable the product idea is and "Development" questions that assess how ready the product idea is from that function's point of view

To use the **Functional Assessments Worksheet**, proceed column-by-column. First, team members determine the importance of all items by rating them on a 0-5 scale. Items rated as a "0" are deemed irrelevant for the project and will not be used in the analysis. Criteria rated as a "5" are critically important to the project. All scores are assigned through discussions with the team. Individuals should not make any ratings alone. The team must share a common understanding of the project.

Next, the team rates each criteria on a 1=Low to 5=High scale from the top of the list to the bottom.

The team then returns to the top of the list to identify SWOT items. This is done by examining the importance and rating scores together. Important items with a high rating may be a strength or an opportunity while important items with low ratings may be a weakness or a threat. Unimportant items are usually not used in a *SWOT Analysis*.

Our first National Science Foundation grant was used to identify information that is knowable and discriminating at an early stage to determine commercial viability.

From this grant we developed the **Functional Assessments Worksheet.** The end result of the *Functional Assessment* is an interdisciplinary view of the commercial viability of your project.

The *Functional Assessment* is a development or elaboration tool. Its use as an evaluation tool should be limited to identifying and correcting problem areas. Note that there are no totals, averages, or cut-off points. The purpose of the *Functional Assessment* is to identify and exploit strong points and to identify and correct problem areas. It provides you with a comprehensive view of the project. Evaluation and comparison of projects for project continuation decisions should use the *Portfolio Evaluation* tool at the end of this chapter.

Functional Assessments Worksheet

MARKETING

Importance	Assessment Criteria	Rating	SWOT

Market Potential

	12345		Strong/Weak	12345	SWOT
1a		Competition - Direct	Strong	Weak	
1b		Competition - Indirect	Strong	Weak	
2		Market allies or partners	None	Numerous	
3		Market size	Small	Large	
4		Expected market share	Small	Large	
5		Market growth	Small	Large	
6		Advantage of product attributes	Limited	Extensive	
7		Relative selling price	High	Low	
8		Portion of a portfolio/platform of related products	Small	Large	
9		Total market size of eventual portfolio	Small	Large	

Market Development

	12345			12345	SWOT
10		Existing channels of distribution	Undeveloped	Developed	
11		Established use	Limited	Extensive	
12		Segment clarity (definability)	Unknown	Defined	
13		Segment desirability	Low	High	
14		Communicability	Difficult	Easy	
15		Trial-ability	Difficult	Easy	
16		Market research ability	Difficult	Easy	
17		Market knowledge of team	Limited	Extensive	

Functional Assessments Worksheet

TECHNOLOGY

Importance	Assessment Criteria	Rating	SWOT

Technology Potential

Importance 12345		Assessment Criteria	Rating 12345		SWOT
1		Performance advantage	None	Superior	
2		Cost / performance advantage	Low	High	
3		Technology base supports a range of products	Limited	Extensive	
4		Range of expertise	Limited	Extensive	

Technology Development

Importance 12345		Assessment Criteria	Rating 12345		SWOT
5		Development strategy and roadmap	None	Developed	
6		Stage of development	Idea	Prototype	
7		Technical feasibility issues identified	Unknown	Clear ID	
8		Cost and/or difficulty of development (complexity)	High	Low	

LEGAL

Legal Potential

Importance 12345		Assessment Criteria	Rating 12345		SWOT
1		Product or process can be patented	No	Yes	
2		Effectiveness of patent protection	Not effective	Effective	
3		Product can be copyright protected	No	Yes	
4		Effectiveness of copyright	Not effective	Effective	
5		Trade secret protection common and effective	Not effective	Effective	

Legal Development

Importance 12345		Assessment Criteria	Rating 12345		SWOT
6		Progress toward patenting	No	Issued	
7		Progress toward copyright	No	Granted	
8		Progress toward trademarking	No	Granted	
9		Information has been kept a trade secret	No	Yes	
10		Technologist is a licensee	Not exclusive	Exclusive	

TEAM/ORGANIZATION

Team / Organization Potential

Importance 12345		Assessment Criteria	Rating 12345		SWOT
1		Entrepreneurial experience	Limited	Extensive	
2		Fit between team skills and project requirements	Weak	Strong	
3		Team stability and history	Weak	Strong	
4		Timing for the team	Poor	Good	

Team / Organization Development

Importance 12345		Assessment Criteria	Rating 12345		SWOT
5		External support (culture)	Limited	Extensive	
6		Technical network	Limited	Extensive	
7		Technical development support	Limited	Extensive	
8		Business network	Limited	Extensive	
9		Business development support	Limited	Extensive	

Functional Assessments Worksheet

OPERATIONS

Importance	Assessment Criteria	Rating	SWOT

Operations Potential

	12345		12345	SWOT
1		Critical items or components are measurable	No — Yes	
2		Standardized skills required to produce	Specialized — Standard	
3		Standardized systems required to produce	Specialized — Standard	
4		Adequacy of supply base	Marginal — Strong	

Operations Development

	12345		12345	SWOT
5		Sufficient quality exists in product	Low — High	
6		Reliable processes established for production	Low — High	
7		Sufficient volumes (scalability and time)	No — Yes	
8		Flexibility to respond to product changes	Low — High	

FINANCE

Financial Potential

	12345		12345	SWOT
1		Product's short-run cash flow potential	Low — High	
2		Product's long-run cash flow potential	Low — High	
3		Product's overall risk level	High — Low	
4		Value of product's real options	Low — High	

Financial Development

	12345		12345	SWOT
5		Access to financial markets and funding sources	Limited — Extensive	
6		Knowledge of total business costs	Unknown — Known	
7		Knowledge of product demand elasticity	Unknown — Known	
8		Knowledge of major financial risks in NPD	Unknown — Known	

If desired, the *Functional Assessment* can be graphically presented. This can be useful to identify areas for improvement and for communicating the status of the project to an interdisciplinary team since each functional area can use this as a common language to discuss the progress of the project.

To chart a project, start by multiplying the importance and rating scores together for each criteria. Then take the average of the potential scores for each functional area. Next, take the average of each development score for each function. Normalize both scores to one.

This will give you six potential scores and six development scores (for each of the six functions) that range from 0 to 1. Then plot the potential by development scores for each function as depicted in Fig. 5-4.

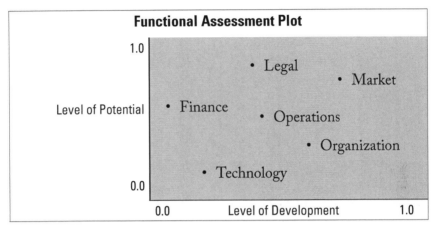

Figure 5-4. The Functional Assessment Plot is a graphic presentation of the Functional Assessment.

Strategic Assessment

The strategic assessment tools are designed to assess the opportunity in terms of its fit with the organization and its competitiveness in the market place. Traditional tools, including *SWOT, Five Forces, Value Chain, Core Competencies,* and *Industry Map,* are used to assess the strategic importance of the opportunity for the company. This helps decision makers recognize, position, and support the new opportunity. Each tool provides a different view of the competitive environment.

Since these are common tools used in most organizations, we assume you already have company-specific versions of them. Therefore, we do not supply System-specific worksheets for these tools.

Strengths, Weaknesses, Opportunities, and Threats (SWOT)

This commonly used analysis provides a good overview of the issues facing any new project. It is simple to use. Strengths and weaknesses are considered descriptive of the company's ability to take advantage of the opportunity. Opportunities and threats are seen as external conditions that affect how well your company can benefit (2).

You can use the following items to start thinking about the SWOT of your opportunity.

Strengths:

- A distinctive competency
- An acknowledged thought leader
- Location advantages
- Intellectual property
- Financial resources to execute plan
- Access to economies of scale
- Cost advantages
- Product innovation capabilities
- Proven management

Weaknesses:

- No clear strategic vision
- Obsolete facilities
- Weak image
- Lagging R&D
- Lack of management depth and talent
- Missing essential skills
- Poor track record
- Operating problems
- Weak marketing skills
- Lack of financial resources

Opportunities:

- Serve multiple customer groups
- Availability of new segments
- Viability of vertical integration
- Barriers to entry for competitors
- Fast market growth
- Lack of competitors
- Installed customer base
- Weak competitors

Threats:

- Likelihood of new competitors
- Likelihood of new regulations
- Slow-to-negative market growth
- Substitute technologies
- Growing strength of customers and suppliers
- Loss of access to distribution channels
- More aggressive management in competition

The items on the SWOT list are often graphically depicted as in Fig. 5-5.

SWOT Analysis

Figure 5-5. SWOT Analysis is used to assess the strategic viability of a project.

Although SWOT analyses have been used for many years, the quality of the analysis partially depends on the amount and quality of the information gathered. The 8-Step method for using Big Data greatly multiplies the value of SWOT by allowing analysts to search vast amounts of information.

Porter's Five Forces Model of Competition

The *Five Forces* model looks beyond your company and competitors to identify external issues facing your innovation. To use the model, identify and list items in each competitive component (3). These issues and what they mean might include:

- Threat of New Entrants: The strength of the barriers to new entrants. Attractiveness of the segment, including growth rate and profit margin.
- Supplier Power: Number and substitutability of suppliers. Your switching costs and the suppliers' ability to forward integrate into your space.
- Buyer Power: Number and criticality of buyers. Buyers' profit margin. Importance of product to buyer.
- Threat of Substitute Products: How easy is it for customers to use some other product or service.
- Inter-firm Rivalry: This is where the action is. While it is important to assess new entrants, suppliers, customers, and substitutes, your competition is often where the greatest threats reside.

Often depicted as shown in Fig. 5-6, the *Five Forces Analysis* is also greatly enhanced with Big Data analytics, which can search unstructured text to reveal information about another company's intensions.

Porter's Five Forces Analysis

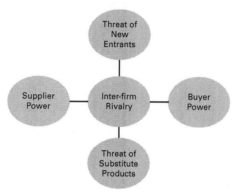

Figure 5-6. Five Forces Analysis will be greatly enhanced by the application of Big Data.

Industry Map

The *Industry Map* identifies the dynamics of inter-firm rivalry. Unlike the *Five Forces* model, the *Industry Map* identifies and names the companies and their relationship to your company for your intended product opportunity.

You enter your company in one of the positions in the competition column (see Fig. 5-7). On the left, you identify the suppliers in the chain you deal with both directly and indirectly. Try to capture the relationship between suppliers and your competitors. For example, some of your competitors may have exclusive agreements with critical suppliers. On the right, you identify the set of distributors that reach your customers. Again, the point is to describe the dynamic relationships between your competitors and your distribution network. Your competition may try to form relationships that block access to important local and international markets.

You should modify the *Industry Map* to capture the situation for your product opportunity. Most *Industry Maps* are complicated, with some players taking multiple positions and conglomerates taking positions in many industries.

Keep in mind there may be a large number of suppliers, competitors, distributors, and customers, and that their existing relationships are likely to be complex, with multiple barriers to keep you out. The point is to describe the competitive landscape and plan how you can enter the industry.

The complexities and subtleties of industry dynamics are particularly amenable to unstructured text analytics. The Big Data process can be used to ascertain the relationships between competitors at each stage in the industry. For example, press releases or industry publications may reveal company announcements about purchasing agreements or opening new facilities. Local news outlets may report on new jobs being created by a competitor in a certain location.

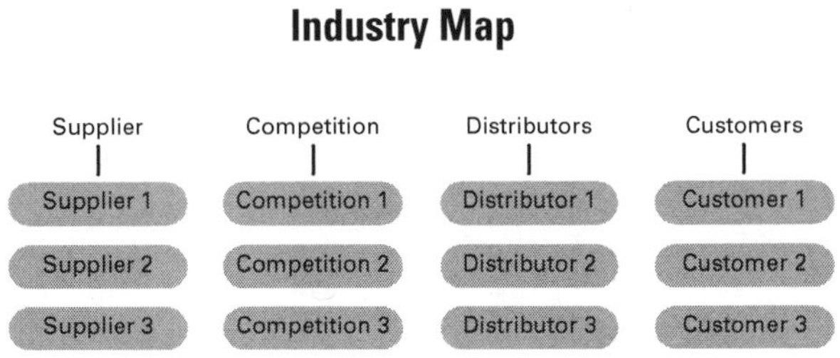

Industry Map

Figure 5-7. The Industry Map sheds light on inter-firm rivalries.

Porter's Value Chain Analysis

The *Value Chain Analysis* is an internal assessment you can use to gauge your firm's capability to deliver the opportunity to your customer. It helps identify what you have and don't have in your company to fulfill your customer's needs with your new opportunity (4).

The Primary Business Processes in Fig. 5-8 directly assess your firm's ability to produce and deliver the intended product. The secondary Support Processes identify the infrastructure necessary to deliver the product. For your project, identify each primary and secondary process needed to satisfy your customers' needs with your new opportunity. Do not include processes and capabilities that don't apply to your project.

Porter's Value Chain

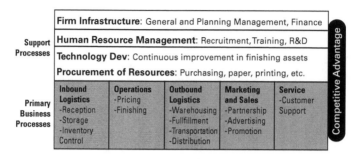

Figure 5-8. Porter's Value Chain Analysis assesses the internal capability of a firm.

Core Competencies

The *Core Competencies* model connects your project to the rest of the firm. It maps the firm's core capabilities, how those are combined into core products and made available to different lines of business, and, finally, how these products can be offered to the market as commercial products and services (see Fig. 5-9).

The challenge is to show decision makers how your opportunity fits the firm's existing core competencies and where there are gaps in its ability to deliver. When it comes to gaps, you will need to provide detailed plans and cost estimates for building the new capability.

Core Competencies Model

Figure 5-9. Top management needs to understand how your opportunity fits the firm's core competencies.

Value Proposition

With all the analyses completed, you are ready to revise the three-sentence

Value Proposition you prepared earlier at the end of Chapter 4, *Module 1: Convert Ideas into Opportunities*. Your updated proposition will be used in **Opportunity Portfolio II** and in developing your business model and case, in the *Develop the Business Case* section below.

Value Proposition Worksheet	
Structure	**Information**
First Sentence	
For (target customer)	
Who (quantified statement of the need or opportunity)	
The (product or service name)	
That (statement of benefit)	
Second Sentence	
Unlike (primary competitive offering)	
Our offering (statement of primary differentiation)	
Third Sentence	
Therefore, we request (give specifics)	

Portfolio Assessment II

The **Portfolio Assessment Worksheet** is the same worksheet found at the end of Chapter 4, *Module 1: Convert Ideas into Opportunities*. In this case, it will help you to decide for which opportunity(s) you will write business cases.

After the opportunity has been elaborated upon and evaluated and the Value Proposition revised, it can again be rated on how well it meets customer needs and the company's ability to deliver. The opportunities are compared to other projects at this stage of development to form a portfolio. Additional portfolio tools can be used to assess ROI, timeliness, risk, and so forth.

Portfolio Assessment Worksheet II

		Ability to Deliver				
		Low			High	
		1	2	3	4	5
Customer Need	High 5					
	4					
	3					
	Low 2					
	1					

Area = size of the opportunity   Color = importance

This second use of the **Opportunity Portfolio Assessment** represents an iteration on the opportunity. The same concept is developed at a deeper level of analysis by using the tools in this chapter.

Develop the Business Case

A business case spells out how the idea is embedded in enduring customer needs and explains how the company can deliver it. The business case has two main parts: (1) a description of the idea and why the intended market will actually buy it and (2) an explanation of how the company can deliver the product to that customer and make a profit. It provides information about needs, customers, and the abilities necessary for making a solid, data-based decision to pursue the opportunity.

The Innovation Project Team assigned by the Innovation Leader will continue to develop the business case.

System for Industrial Innovation

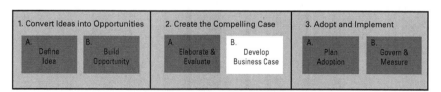

Figure 5-10. The business case identifies the critical elements necessary to make sound decisions to proceed with development.

A business case is *not* the same as a business plan. The case is a document that provides the needed information and analyses for decision makers to make well-informed funding decisions. The business plan, on the other hand, is the outcome of deeper, more thorough analyses and planning. Whereas the business plan addresses all facets of delivering a new opportunity to the market, the business case focuses on critical elements necessary to make sound decisions to proceed with development.

The elaboration and evaluation of the opportunity provides the content necessary to write the business case. That content should tell a story about why the opportunity is unique and believable. Content from the *Elaborate and Evaluate* step is also used to describe how the company will be able to manufacture and/or deliver the product at the time, place, price, quantity, and quality acceptable to customers and at a cost commensurate with the company's ability to deliver at a sustainable profit.

The **Business Case Worksheet** gathers all the pertinent information in one place to assess the strength of the logic and sufficiency of the information. Even though the business case focuses on only the critical issues everyone recognizes, the opportunity must address all the issues. This creates a dilemma. Try to explain everything and you risk losing support because people get lost in the detail and conclude that you can't distinguish and focus on the critical elements. Fail to address all the issues? You risk people thinking you have missed something important.

The **Business Case Worksheet** resolves this dilemma. This worksheet identifies all issues—critical and mundane—necessary to implementing the opportunity.

By viewing them in a formatted template, you can quickly acknowledge the status of every issue without completely planning for each item.

The worksheet allows you to examine all issues and make a statement about the degree of importance and risk associated with each issue. Reviewers and decision makers who disagree with the assessment can respond by elevating an item to critical status.

In this worksheet, Strategic Fit and Market Need (or Problem Being Solved) are two of the critical elements of the business case. These items likely require the most attention. Of course, your project may have different critical elements. The level of criticality is determined by your research and in discussion with the decision makers or their staffs. Similarly, there may be other elements you need to add to the template.

Business Case Worksheet			
Step	**Explanation**	**Project Specific Information**	**Action Items**
1. Executive Summary	What is the project, how is it unique?		
2. Value Proposition	The target market's needs, your project characteristics and competitive advantage		
3. Business Model	How the company aligns the opportunity with the factors of production to make a profit		
4.a. Critical Element: Strategic Fit	How does the project fit with the intended direction and objectives of the adopting business unit?		
4.b. Critical Element: Market Need (problem being solved)	Will the intended customers accept the product? How are they benefitted?		
5.a. Other Elements: Ability	What abilities are required and where can they be found?		
5.b. Other Elements: Suppliers	Who outside the company will be involved and how will they react?		
5.c. Other Elements: Recommended Approach	How will the idea be demonstrated to be viable? What will it take to convince the decision makers this is possible? Project management details.		
5.d. Other Elements: IP Plan	A clear plan for "freedom to operate" or intellectual property protection.		
5.e. Other Elements: Project Risks	What risks and uncertainties are there and how can they be mitigated?		

Business Case Worksheet			
5.f. Other Elements: Recruitment	Availability and location of needed talent.		
6. Timeline	When will the project start, what are the major milestones and when will it be completed?		
7. Financial Projections	How much will it cost and how much will the company gain?		
8. Adoption Plan	How is the project going to proceed? Who will be needed to provide support, resources, and decisions to further the project in different phases of development?		

Executive Summary

The executive summary highlights the information managers must know before making a decision. Depending on the industry, competitors, intellectual property, and so forth, different elements will be critical to each project.

The worksheet provides prompts to help you organize information that is typically sought at this stage of business case development.

Executive Summary Worksheet	
Value Proposition	
Uniqueness	
Benefit	
Reason to Believe	
Key Statistics	

Value Proposition

A business case must focus on the primary forces driving the success of your project, which are reflected in the following questions: (1) What are the major factors that convince you that your opportunity will make a profit?, (2) What makes you sure that your customers will need and buy your product?, and (3) What makes you sure you will receive the needed investment? These points are succinctly stated in the **Value Proposition Worksheet** at the end of Chapter 4, *Module 1: Convert Ideas into Opportunities* and again at the end of the first section of this chapter.

The Value Proposition you have already developed gets used here as part of the content of your business case. It describes the customers, their specific needs, the offering and its unique feature, and reasons to believe in the offering's viability. It also identifies the resources needed to commercialize it.

The many possible Value Propositions fall into three main categories: (1) lower cost, (2) higher performance, and (3) new capabilities required. A Value Proposition must relate directly to the organization's strategy; it is not some "cool" technology. Instead, the Value Proposition must capture the enduring customer need and the firm's ability to deliver it. Creating a Value Proposition is an exercise in communicating that value succinctly.

It's important to distinguish the Value Proposition from other strategic documents. While the Value Proposition addresses the what, who, and why of a new offering, the Business Model answers how the value proposition will be exploited. Then there is the Business Case, which tackles the additional dimensions of where, when, cost, and profit.

Business Model

The Business Model is the part of the Business Case that explains how the organization will capture value from the opportunity. The Business Model starts by inputting the value proposition developed in Module 1, revised in Module 2, and used in the **Executive Summary Worksheet.** We then use Osterwalder, Pigneur, and Clark's nine-box model, *Generating Business Models,* as the tool to create the Business Model (5).

The *Business Model Canvas* in Fig. 5-11 (Osterwalder, Pigneur, and Clark's nine-box model) assumes you have a Value Proposition that you offer to customer segments. The work should have already been done to focus on the customer segments. The model then helps you identify the nature of the relationship that needs to be developed with the customer; maybe it's personal assistance or automated service. In the Business Model Canvas, you also select the channel you will use to deliver your offering. The right side of the canvas ends by specifying your revenue stream, which could include asset sales, licenses, services, and the like.

The boxes on the left side of the Business Model Canvas identify key elements necessary to meet the customers' needs. These activities include identifying the key resources and partnerships needed as core capabilities for delivering the product to customers. These activities and resources drive the cost structure.

Understanding and specifying the relationship between these boxes determines your Business Model. For example, if your Value Proposition is aimed at a new mobile phone subscription for, say, a service that updates users on waiting times at local restaurants, you might have a mass customer segment approach where your relationship with customers is electronically rather than personally mediated. Your revenue stream comes from monthly subscription fees. To deliver this service to the intended customer segment, you need to identify your key activities, such as programming and sales, as well as the resources needed to execute those activities. You will also need to partner with phone service providers and specify the price for delivering the service.

Building Business Models identifies a number of generic models to start thinking about your business model. It is often beneficial to try casting your opportunity as other business models.

- Unbundling
- Open Model
- Long Tail
- Multi-sided Platform

- Bait and Hook
- Free/Freemium

Business Model Canvas

Business Model Canvas	Designed For		Designed By	
Key Partners • Who are our Key Partners? • Who are our Key Suppliers? • Which Key Resources are we acquiring from partners? • Which Key Activities do partners perform? Motivation for partnerships: • Optimization and economy • Reduction of risk and uncertainty • Acquisition of particular resources and activities	**Key Activities** • What Key Activities do our Value Propositions require? • Our Distribution Channels • Customer Relationships • Revenue streams? Categories • Production • Problem Solving • Platform/Network **Key Resources** • What Key Resources do our Value Propositions require? • Our Distribution Channels • Customer Relationships • Revenue Streams Types of resources • Physical • Intellectual (brand patents, copyrights, data) • Human • Financial	**Value Proposition** • What value do we deliver to the customer? • Which one of our customer's problems are we helping to solve? • What bundles of products and services are we offering to each Customer Segment? • Which customer needs are we satisfying? Characteristics • Newness • Performance • Customization • "Getting the Job Done" • Design • Brand/Status • Price • Cost Reduction • Risk Reduction • Accessibility • Convenience/Usability	**Customer Relationships** • What type of relationships does each of our Customer Segments expect us to establish and maintain with them? • Which one have we established? • How are they integrated with the rest of our business model? • How costly are they? Examples • Personal assistance • Dedicated Personal Assistance • Self-Service • Automated Services • Communities • Co-creation **Channels** • Through which Channels do our Customer Segments want to be reached? • How are we reaching them now? How are our Channels integrated? • Which ones work best? • Which ones are most cost-efficient? • How are we integrating them with customer routines? Channel phases: 1. Awareness 2. Evaluation 3. Purchase 4. Delivery 5. After sales	**Customer Segments** • For whom are we creating value? • Who are our most important customers? Market Types • Mass Market • Niche Market • Segmented • Diversified Multi-sided • Platform

| **Cost Structure**

• What are the most important costs inherent in our business model?
• Which Key Resources are most expensive?
• Which Key Activities are most expensive?

Is your business more:

• Cost Driven (leanest cost structure, low price value proposition, maximum automation, extensive outsourcing)
• Value Driven (focused on value creation, premium value proposition)
Sample Characteristics:
• Fixed Costs (salaries, rents utilities) • Variable costs • Economies of scale • Economies of scope | **Revenue Streams**

• For what value are our customers really willing to pay?
• For what do they currently pay?
• How are they currently paying?
• How would they prefer to pay?
• How much does each Revenue Stream contribute to overall revenues?

Types:
• Asset sale   • Usage fee
• Lending/Renting/Leasing Licensing Brokerage fees   • Subscription fee
• Advertising |

Figure 5-11. Business Model Canvas can help you describe the relationship.

The bottom line is this: The Business Model explains how your company makes a profit from the opportunity. It forces you to specify whose needs you are addressing, the specific nature of those needs, how you will deliver your solution to those customers, and how you will get paid for it. Again, we see the idea embedded in enduring customer needs and the ability to deliver as the critical equation to solve.

Business Models are not resource-neutral. It takes time and effort to address new market segments and conduct key activities. The Business Model Canvas specifies the revenue and cost models but does not address where the resources come from to invest in the new model. The Innovation Leader, along with the functional heads, must decide on a funding model. Most organizations have a limit on the number of people they can hire. Therefore, new projects, particularly major ones, cannot just be distributed among current staff. Decisions about new or reassigned resources must be part of the overall decision-making process.

At some point, it might become obvious that other parts of the organization could be cut to take advantage of the new project. Often, significant savings can be gained by reassigning resources from redundant or commodity-like activities to higher value innovations.

Critical Elements

The Business Case tells management which elements of the project are critical to success and where to focus further development. Every project should be assessed for critical elements.

Ideally, you have identified the critical elements in the *Functional* and *Strategic Assessments* carried out in the *Elaborate and Evaluate* section of this module. For example, a project with a market item in the functional assessment that is highly important but has a low score could be critical.

Here's a partial list of frequently encountered critical elements:

- Market acceptance
- Strategic fit and priorities
- Available capital
- Intellectual property
- Channels of distribution
- Available partners
- Political conflicts

- Competition
- Production costs
- Materials costs
- Qualified personnel
- Regulatory risks
- Profitability
- Longevity

The point is not to address all these issues—the Business Plan will do that—but rather to identify and deal with the critical elements upon which the success of the project rests. Most projects will have between one to four critical elements that, when successfully addressed, will likely enable the project to go forward. These issues are usually substantial and require some resolution before further investment can be justified.

Market Acceptance

In many cases, market acceptance is a critical issue that must be addressed. The primary market questions include the size and growth of the target market and how likely prospective customers are to buy the product. The **Market Size Worksheet** is designed to help answer market-acceptance questions.

Market Size Worksheet	
Item	**Description**
Market Description without you in it. Segments, trends, size	
Customer needs assessment (e.g., VOC)	
Market Positioning (PAMM cells)	
Value Proposition	
Sales Model: Entry and expansion, sales cycle, identify first 100 customers	
Competitor Reaction	
Market Size = Adoption Rate (P of 4/5) X Addressable Market X Price	See the "Rule of 4s and 5s" in the Finance Section

Strategic Fit and Priorities

Another critical issue that arises, particularly for those breakthrough innovations, is how the project aligns with your firm's strategies and business priorities. This is critical because the new project must compete for resources and support. The tools in the strategic assessment section are used to assess the current strategies and to demonstrate how the new opportunity provides competitive advantage to the firm.

Other Elements

Other elements of the Business Case include those non-essential issues that will eventually be in the business plan, but they are worth noting if they impact the success of the project. It is important to distinguish between critical and non-critical elements. If you present decision makers with complete information at this stage, they are likely to feel overloaded and be unable to make a timely decision. Reveal only enough about each of these other elements to show decision makers that you recognize the issue for what it is. Persuade them that these elements are likely not critical. Other elements can often be presented in a simple table like the **Business Case Worksheet.** If the decision makers disagree about what is critical, you must resolve those disagreements before seeking formal approval.

Timeline

Timing is an important issue for every new idea. Decision makers naturally want to know how long it will take to develop and introduce the opportunity into the company or market and when they can expect to see the promised benefits. This is difficult, particularly if the project includes R&D or open innovation. These activities are event- rather than calendar-driven.

The challenge for project proponents is to synchronize event and calendar time to make the project predictable enough so that management can determine the risk and make an informed decision. Projects with unknown risks should never be funded.

You should prepare a timeline that includes development milestones, market events, and financial commitments. This can take many forms, but a simple Gantt Chart such as the one shown in Fig. 5-12 will usually suffice.

Product Development Gantt Chart

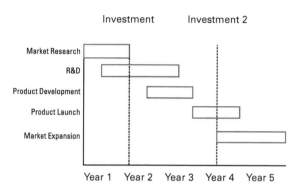

Figure 5-12. Timelines should be developed for every project.

Finances

One of the most difficult parts of writing a Business Case is estimating the project's impact on your company. This is especially difficult for projects aimed at gaining new sales for new products and markets. It is important to understand that the financial estimates are the end result of all your previous work. If you have been careful to validate your market needs, competitor reactions, and operational costs in the previous sections, your financial estimates will be more believable.

The **Financial Estimate Worksheet** provides a method for identifying and presenting financial estimates most often questioned by decision makers. The estimates in the worksheet may or may not be appropriate for your particular project. You must be careful to modify the worksheet to match your project.

A word on using spreadsheets to make estimates: Revenues are too often arrived at through "spreadsheet abuse." This is the common practice of assuming a certain percentage of the market will buy your offering, then taking a percent of a percent for sales growth, and then taking a percent of that number to reduce the estimate to make the revenue projection conservative. Rather than being conservative, this is an admission of ignorance. One should never, ever present financial information based on presumed market share and/or an assumed percentage of growth and discounts.

Each line of the Worksheet is described below. Note that the financial estimates are prepared for multiple years depending on the industry. Software may only need three years, while capital-intensive projects might require seven or more years. It is important that you talk with your finance department to agree on how many years are appropriate. The amount of time in which your project is expected to pay back the investment and produce profits is critical to the value of the opportunity.

Financial Estimate Worksheet					
	Year 1	Year 2	Year 3	Year 4	Year 5
1. Head count					
2. Impact on overhead					
3. Addressable Market Segments: 1, 2, 3, . . . (Size)					
4. Adoption Rate (4s & 5s)					
5. Price					
6. Revenue (Market Segment X Rate X Price)					
7. Capital Expense					
8. Operating Expense					
9. Contribution					

1. Head Count. The number of people in the organization has a major impact on financial estimates. Rules of thumb for different industries relate the number of employees to both the expenses and revenues of the firm and, by extension, can be used for your project. For example, if the full cost of an employee is $250,000 per year, the cost estimates for your project should be close to that or a compelling reason given for why that is not the case. Similarly, if revenues are $400,000 per year per employee, you must provide a reason why it is substantially different for your project.

The number of people you estimate will be involved in your project should be related to the amount of work called for in your plan.

You lose credibility if your estimates are too high or low or if the financial impact of headcount is vastly different from the rest of the company without justification.

2. Impact on Overhead. It is important to assure decision makers that the delivery of your project will not adversely impact

overhead. In particular, if overhead expenses are converted into delivery resources, this needs to be made clear. For example, if the new product requires extensive IT support, then you should clearly indicate that overhead costs would increase.

3. Addressable Market Segments. This should come from the work you have already done in the *Product Attribute and Market Matrix*. The Business Model should identify segments. It may make sense to designate an advantageous segment as the entry strategy and other segments as expansion strategies. The important aspect to identify in the **Financial Estimate Worksheet** at this point is the size of the market in terms of potential customers.

4. Adoption Rate. This is the most difficult figure to obtain. At this early stage of development, we use the Rule of 4s and 5s to determine the percentage of customers in a given segment who are likely to buy your new offering at the intended price.

Rule of 4s and 5s

> 1. Identify and quantify the target entry segment.
>
> 2. Present the product concept with the price to an entry-segment sample.
>
> 3. Solicit an intention to buy on a scale of 1-5 (1=Low and 5=High)
>
> 4. Add together the percent of people who answered 4 or 5; this percentage becomes your initial adoption rate.

This procedure offers decision makers some evidence that the revenue figures are based on actual customers' intentions to buy given a set of product features and price. This is only an early-stage estimate, and, while helpful, it's not a replacement for more analysis during preparation of a complete business plan. You may need to repeat the procedure for different price points or feature sets and for each market segment.

5. Price. Pricing is a difficult strategic activity, requiring as much contact with customers as the initial needs and product research. There are numerous methods to establish the price of your offering. You should pick one, two, or three of the following methods to substantiate your price. Note that your price point is also substantiated using the Rule of 4s & 5s.

- Comparisons: Price set to be the same as similar offerings.

- Market: Price determined by what the market would bear.

- Cost Plus: The final price is the result of cost recovery plus a set profit margin.

- Portfolio: Price is determined by its position in the portfolio.

- Volume: Price dependent on the volume of units purchased.

- Features: Price determined by the number of features in the offering.

- Value Add: Price determined by recognizing how much value your offering adds.

- Regulatory: Some prices are set through regulations or payment schedules.

- 3rd Party Payer: Some prices set by third parties, such as insurance companies.

- Free: You make your money elsewhere in the relationship you are building.

- Razor Blade: Price set artificially low and charge for consumption.

6. Revenue. At this point, calculating revenue should be straightforward. Multiply the addressable market by the adoption rate and by the price. Revenue for one time period is easily calculated. The validity of the revenue projection depends on the rigor of the work done to determine market, adoption, and price information. Even though you have calculated a preliminary adoption rate, estimating revenue is not as simple as multiplying the adoption rate by the market size for following years. You must also consider the sales cycle and length of time it takes a customer to decide to buy. You should also model the number of sales people you are able to employ and train in a given year and what their expected performance will be. For example, if you have only enough resources to cover 10 percent of the market in the first year, and it takes six months to hire and train sales people, you can multiply your adoption rate by at most five percent.

These practicalities of sales must be taken into account to estimate revenue.

7. Capital Expenses. Identify any capital purchases that need to be made, including any long-term expenses likely to be incurred. Patent rights, royalty payments, or other large expenses should be identified.

8. Operating Expenses. From the business model you should be able to identify any differences between your project's operating expenses and the company norm. Of course, decision makers are looking for the highest possible ratio of revenue over operating expenses given the capital expense.

9. Contribution. Describe and quantify the contribution you anticipate your project will bring to your company. The contribution could be financial, reputational, competitive, internal (for example, employee satisfaction), or any other valuable benefit.

Breakeven Analysis

The important information from proforma financial statements is contained in a breakeven analysis. The initial investment is plotted on the Y-axis of Fig. 5-13. The project may operate at a loss for some time. However, the new offering will, at some point, become cash flow positive, meaning it starts to earn more money than it costs. It is not until all the investment and operating loss is earned back that the project is said to break even.

The point when this happens is very important to decision makers because it represents the amount of time they will be exposed to risk.

The most important part of the breakeven analysis, however, is the profit or benefit section. This is the payoff for taking the risk. But because it is difficult to know the size of a possible future payoff, decision makers will often not believe your estimate and will consequently discount it. It's much easier to see the immediate investment risk and the possible loss than to imagine a payoff that might be years away. The System's tools are designed to add credibility to future estimates. This is why it's imperative you do all the work the System calls for.

Breakeven Analysis

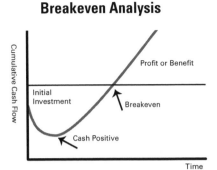

Figure 5-13. A breakeven analysis incorporates information from your proforma statements.

Adoption

Business Cases don't often include information about how the project will be adopted. Nevertheless, most decision makers will question how the new project will impact other parts of the organization. Because this has a large impact on project approval decisions, we include it in the Business Case and discuss it here.

How projects get adopted is a major concern for anyone who has laboriously developed a project only to see it die from inaction by the rest of the organization. Explicit treatment of this painful subject is frequently omitted from both Business Cases and Business Plans. The Valley of Death is a metaphor for getting projects accepted, both internally and externally. The critical part of the metaphor is adoption by the rest of the organization, not just idea development.

That is why *Module 3* is devoted to adoption and implementation of the opportunity. In preparing the Business Case, you must prove that there are no fatal organizational, technical, or market blocks or other fatal flaws. This is accomplished by proactively defining roles and responsibilities in the earliest stages of development for all the constituents affected by the project. Unfortunately, idea proponents often anticipate resistance and attempt to isolate themselves from the criticism of presumed opponents. While there is definitely merit to developing an idea to the point where it is solid before opening it up to scrutiny, the longer the project is protected, the more opposition can be expected. It takes much more work to resolve these issues after the idea has become widely known.

That's why your Business Case should identify all potential conflicts with other parts of the organization, especially other business units that serve the same customers and might not want any interference, even in the form of improved products. Opposition can come in the form of competition for scarce resources regardless of the value of your project. Often projects are just the victim of apathy and lack of interest.

Information from the **Roles and Responsibilities Worksheet** (in Chapter 6, *Module 3: Adopt and Implement*) should be used in the Business Case. It incorporates the model for crossing the Valley of Death by defining the people who should be involved and what you want them to do. The timing of each person's involvement is critically important. Consider carefully when you want people to be involved and be specific about what you need them to do.

Chapter 6, *Module 3: Adopt and Implement* is designed to take the Business Case from a document to action. Focusing on how the organization will manage it and hold people accountable is critical for all projects.

The first half of Chapter 6 details how to plan for the project's adoption. The second half discusses how to implement innovation projects and measure results.

REFERENCES FOR CHAPTER 5

1. Mankins, J.C. 1995. "Technology Readiness Levels." White Paper, Office of Space Access and Technology, NASA.

2. Barney, J. 1991. "Firm Resources and Sustained Competitive Advantage." *Journal of Management*, 17: 99-120.

3. Porter, M.E. 2008. "The Five Competitive Forces that Shape Strategy." *Harvard Business Review*, 86: 25-40.

4. Porter, M.E. 1987. "From Competitive Advantage to Corporate Strategy." *Harvard Business Review*, 65: 43-59.

5. Osterwalder, A., Pigneur, Y., and Clark, T. 2010. *Business Model Generation: A Handbook for Visionaries, Game Changers, and Challengers*. Wiley, Hoboken, New Jersey.

Notes:

Module 3: Adopt and Implement

Make Decisions

As essential as the compelling Business Case is, it is just the start of the process of adopting and implementing your opportunity. The Business Case is a core requirement for selling decision-makers on the opportunity's value to the company. Unfortunately, too many innovators see completing the Business Case as the end of the process when it is simply the tool for climbing out of the Valley of Death. Implementing the project across the whole organization is actually a much bigger task.

A compelling Business Case provides the talking points for convincing many people and departments across the organization to seriously consider and even start to plan for and implement the new project. Some support may be generated while writing the case, but you will have to continue to work hard throughout the decision and implementation process to gain the necessary support from the rest of the organization.

Seek final approval from senior management only when you have gained that support and overcome, or at least defused, the inevitable opposition. As we like to say: *Never go into a decision meeting looking for a decision.* If the decision has not been made before the meeting, then find a way to cancel the meeting. Seriously, if you're not certain of approval, change the nature of the meeting to an information meeting; you could also postpone the meeting or use it to seek top management's guidance. If you value your work, you will not go into a meeting seeking a decision without knowing what will happen.

Adoption Plan

Module 3 provides the tools and metrics for getting your business opportunity adopted and the necessary innovation capabilities institutionalized within the organization. In *Module 3A: Plan Adoption,* the team leverages the value of the project as it plans for its adoption by the rest of organization. Finally, the team optimizes the project by carrying out the activities in *Module 3B: Govern and Measure.*

Involving other people and parts of the organization in breakthrough innovation projects will require specific requests and actions at the appropriate times. The adoption planning tools help you embed your innovation activities within the organization's governance structure and metrics.

System for Industrial Innovation

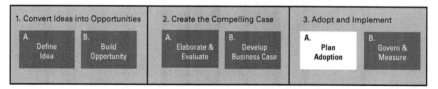

Figure 6-1. Coordinated adoption planning is essential for successful implementation.

Too often, the act of getting a project adopted is left to chance, with little to no planning or effort exerted to encourage people to embrace a new idea or opportunity. Without a coordinated adoption plan, all your earlier innovation efforts are likely to go unrewarded.

Fortunately, adoption, like all innovation activities, is a manageable process. But it requires knowledge of adoption methods and forethought about each project.

The following tools will increase your chances of getting an opportunity adopted:

- **Adoption Worksheet**: This worksheet helps you identify and manage the many activities involved in getting a large organization to adopt a new project.
- **Roles and Responsibilities Worksheet**: This worksheet identifies who will be involved with the project, what their contribution will be, and when it is needed.
- **Stakeholder Action Plan Worksheet**: This worksheet identifies all the people affected by the project, what their reactions might be, and how to resolve any problems. Decisions and action plans to respond to all issues surface in the Stakeholder Analysis.
- **Adoption Timeline**: This tool identifies all the major activities and milestones.
- **Communication Architecture**: This tool helps you identify all the people you need to talk to and what you need to communicate to them.
- **Decision-Ready Checklist Worksheet**: This worksheet helps you prepare for decision-making meetings

Adoption Worksheet

Adoption is a multifaceted endeavor involving diverse activities and people. Keeping track of everything that needs to be done is difficult. Any single task can consume a great deal of time and energy, causing people to lose track of other activities. The **Adoption Worksheet** helps to identify and track the completion of everything required to facilitate adoption. Use it to manage all the other steps in the adoption plan.

Adoption Worksheet				
Task	Start Date	End Date	Person Assigned	Notes
Completed Business Case				
Role and Responsibilities				
Stakeholder Analysis & Action Plan				
Adoption Time Line				
Communication Architecture				
Decision Ready Checklist				

Roles and Responsibilities

As soon as the idea is identified, you should start locating the stakeholders and anyone else who is needed to advance the project through the Valley of Death.

Roles and Responsibilities Worksheet				
	Breakthrough Innovation	Valley of Death	Formal Development	Adoption
Innovation Executive	Vision	Resources	Program Acceptance	Adoption
Innovation Manager	Initiate	Manage	Transfer Projects	
Project Leader	Feasibility	Protection	Develop	Promotion
Recipient Representative	Participate in Ideation		Project Reviews	Lead Adoption into Unit
Recipient Executive			Development Resources	Adoption Planning, Metrics
Development Manager			Accept and Develop Projects	Transfer to Adopting Unit
Development Team		Assess Project	Conduct Work	Transfer to Adopting Unit

Using the **Roles and Responsibilities Worksheet,** you first identify the roles needed for your project from the very start all the way through to commercialization. Next, the responsibilities for each role are assigned to the appropriate person, along with the allotted time and order in which the activities will be carried out.

Stakeholder Action Plan

The Stakeholder Analysis (Fig. 6-2) is the basis for identifying actions necessary to get a project adopted. The **Stakeholder Action Plan Worksheet** defines and structures everything that needs to be done for project adoption. In addition to identifying the people needed for adoption, the plan requires knowing who else will be affected by the project and what impact they might have on it. Within the Business Case is a set of activities and needed resources that are connected to people with control over them. These people are included at the beginning of a Stakeholder Analysis. Additional people who will be affected by the project—both inside and outside the organization—are also identified.

The Stakeholder Analysis is conducted as follows:

- Identify all the stakeholders.
- Learn how they will be impacted by your project.
- Through conversation, assess their reaction to the impact.
- Decide who will be responsible for responding to those concerns and how this will be done.

Stakeholder Analysis

Figure 6-2. A Stakeholder Analysis will tell you which actions–and people–are necessary to get your project adopted.

At the conclusion of the Stakeholder Analysis, list your responses to the expressed concerns on the **Stakeholder Action Plan Worksheet**. Although you may not make everyone happy with these responses, every stakeholder concern must be addressed and communicated back to them.

The Stakeholder Action Plan allows you to organize, assign, and track those responses.

Stakeholder Action Plan Worksheet						
Stakeholder	Expected Impact	Response (Action items)	Person Assigned	Start Date	End Date	Feedback Date and Notes

Adoption Timeline

You should develop an adoption timeline that incorporates the timeline from the Business Case, which includes the commercialization activities but adds decision-making and internal sales. It should also include resource acquisition, time to develop external partnerships, and other adoption activities.

Timelines can take a variety of forms. Anything from simple lists to charts in spreadsheets to specialized project-management software can be used to visually communicate when the various activities will start and stop. This is particularly important for decision makers as they can clearly see the resources and amount of time they can expect to invest in the project. Of course, it is critical to coordinate the activities of other project participants, too.

In addition to the start and finish times of sub-tasks, the timeline should identify everyone who is involved as well as when various investments must be made for the project to continue.

The timeline substantiates the **Roles and Responsibilities Worksheet** and, by extension, the detailed managerial plan for crossing the Valley of Death.

Communication Architecture

For a project to be adopted, its advocates must communicate relevant information to many people. This can be a big chore; if not managed comprehensively, it can be all too easy for project advocates to overlook information that can help them convince the company to embrace a new opportunity. Therefore, a comprehensive plan must be used to identify who needs what information and when, presented in a user-friendly format.

To build such a communication architecture (see Fig 6-3), you must decide:

- What are the objectives of the communications?
- Who are the communication targets?
- Which targets are likely to be responsive to which features of the project?
- What messages are you communicating to each target?
- What method will you use to communicate that message?
- When and how often will you communicate?

Communication Architecture					
Targets of Communication	**Messages**				
	Technology update	*Partner progress*	*Market research*	*Financial performance*	*Patent progress*
Project manager	Monthly report	Quarterly report	Monthly report	Monthly report	Monthly report
Business Unit Executive	Online newsletter	Online newsletter	Monthly report	Monthly report	Quarterly email
Partner manager	Quarterly report				Quarterly report
Internal Attorney	Monthly report				Monthly report
Marketing Manager			Monthly report	Monthly report	
Cells = Modes and frequencies of communication					

Figure 6-3. A communication architecture shows what information must be communicated as well as to whom and when.

Project advocates often struggle with choosing an appropriate communication method. Therefore, we present a simple model in Fig. 6-4 that will help you choose the appropriate communication tool for your situation. Decide on both the level of specificity and the degree of interaction you desire. Then choose the tool corresponding to how you prefer to communicate.

Modes of Communication

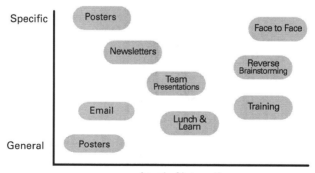

Figure 6-4. Suggested communication modes from which to choose.

Decision-Ready Checklist

Decision makers are very busy, and their schedules are so fragmented that they often do not have the dedicated time to thoroughly review important information. They may not do the necessary homework, such as talking to others or thinking through implications. Similarly, the proposers may not have thought about how to actually elicit a decision. They might not have provided enough information or presented it in a way that can be used to make clear decisions.

Making decisions about innovations is notoriously tricky. People do not always know who has the authority to commit to a new opportunity. The more the project impacts other team members across the organization, the murkier the decision becomes.

Also, the criteria for innovation project decisions are often hard to pin down. By definition, the new project does not conform to existing practices.

The **Decision-Ready Checklist Worksheet** is a tool for preparing both the presenter and the decision maker(s) to make a decision.

Use the checklist by following these directions:

1. Identify all the decision makers needed to move the project to the next step.

2. State the decision you need them to make.

3. Present all the information necessary for their decision.

4. Revise the plans and/or decision.

5. Record the decision.

6. State the actions to be taken.

Decision-Ready Checklist Worksheet				
Project Objective:			Meeting Date:	
Decision Makers	Decision	Information Provided	Pre-meeting Discussion	Issues Noted
1				
2				
3				
4				
5				
Decisions Made:				
Next Actions:				

Govern and Measure

All the adoption-planning actions in the first part of this chapter are required to move an idea from the business case to implementation. Rather than just focusing on individual projects, these innovation actions should be part of ongoing operations. Making innovation a core capability of the organization requires capturing and systematizing those efforts so they can be repeated reliably. The govern and measure activities in Fig. 6-5 are accomplished in two ways: (1) implementing governance procedures that establish the legitimacy of the innovation effort, which depends on a visible line of authority from CEO to the innovation activities and empowers people to support innovation efforts and (2) creating and applying metrics that measure both activity and performance of the breakthrough innovation program.

Innovation systems must be permanently embedded in the organization. Otherwise, individual projects and even the entire innovation program may soon lose support and legitimate standing, thereby becoming less effective and ultimately cancelled for lack of performance.

This would be an unfortunate outcome given that the bigger failure is not managing innovation as a core organizational competency.

System for Industrial Innovation

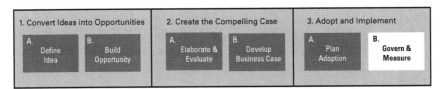

Figure 6-5. Governance procedures must be implemented to permanently embed innovation in the organization.

Embedding innovation in the organization requires making a set of decisions about how centralized the innovation system will be. Will the effort be in a central location or distributed among the business units? Will it be centrally controlled or made responsive to customers? Questions like these lead to a decision about ambidexterity: the extent to which the organization's innovation activities are separated from its day-to-day operations. In general, the more innovative the intended results, the greater the separation must be. This in turn creates another problem: how to integrate the results back into the organization.

According to O'Connor's systems approach, embedding innovation in your organization depends on making decisions about the following aspects of your innovation system (1):

- **Scope and Focus.** Management must decide on the program size, strategic priorities, desired impact, and availability of resources. Breakthrough innovation programs should be funded at 10 to 20 percent of the R&D budget (2).

- **Organizational Structure.** Companies must establish where the innovation efforts fit into the organization. Many times innovation responsibilities are given to already-busy people while maintaining the existing reporting relationships. This automatically isolates those people and their activities. Overloading staff members is a common occurrence that compels them to establish their own priorities for dealing with insurmountable tasks. A structure with clean boundaries, appropriate resources, and strong leadership and reporting relationships is necessary.

- **Interfaces.** How the innovation efforts interact with the rest of the organization must be made explicit. All parties to innovation efforts must agree on what they will need from the rest of the organization and what they will give back.

113

- **Exploratory Processes.** Innovation systems must include exploratory processes that seek market needs and sources of solutions both internally and externally. These processes must be well developed, taught extensively, and implemented with rigor.

- **Skills Development.** Complex innovation activities will not manage themselves. Innovation is a learned set of behaviors carried out jointly by many people at different levels in the organization; therefore, skills training at both the management and staff levels is essential.

- **Governance.** Decisions about innovation program goals and how performance will be monitored must be agreed upon. In addition, adequate resources must be allocated, the portfolio must be reviewed periodically and continuation decisions made, training must be conducted, and talented leadership must be assigned.

- **Performance Metrics.** Because innovation outcomes can be long term, it is essential to measure activity and performance in order to be certain the program is doing the right things. This is particularly important at the start of the program to ensure the outcomes will not be delayed as leadership gropes for direction.

- **Leadership.** A leadership structure is necessary so that people know who is responsible, how to contact the innovation program, and who is accountable. The leadership aligns innovation and strategy, owns the exploratory process, and establishes and monitors outcomes and activity metrics.

The System provides the following three mechanisms for carrying out these activities effectively:

- Innovation Portfolio Committee
- Measure and Improve
- Innovation Management Maturity Assessment

Innovation Structure

Innovation Committees provide an effective way for organizations to balance the need to separate innovation activities while also integrating their results. Innovation Committees are permanent structures that integrate all the embedding actions described above in one organizational structure (3, 4). Committees have both permanent and temporary members to flexibly start and stop projects. They also act as a network to connect resources and stakeholders.

We expand the Innovation Committees concept for use in the System with the creation of the Innovation Portfolio Committee (IPC). The IPC is a permanent structure that reports to the Innovation Leader. The IPC works on individual opportunities by establishing temporary Innovation Project Teams, as seen in Fig. 6-6.

Innovation Project Team Structure

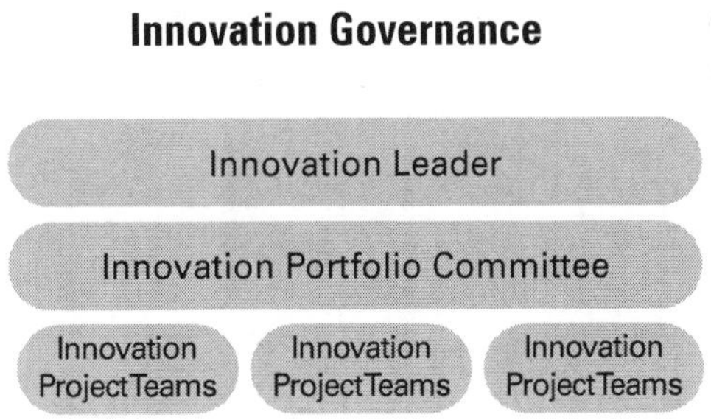

Innovation Governance

Innovation Leader

Innovation Portfolio Committee

| Innovation Project Teams | Innovation Project Teams | Innovation Project Teams |

Figure 6-6. From his/her position atop the innovation structure, the Innovation Leader provides top-down guidance to innovate.

Innovation Leader

The IPC is led by an Innovation Leader who, as mentioned in Chapter 1, *Introduction*, is central to the System. The title and position of these individuals varies widely, but what they have in common is a driving passion to make improvements in the organization. Innovation Leaders are usually experienced and influential. It is also important they be senior people who have direct access to the top decision makers. Innovation requires both bottom-up and top-down effort; the Innovation Leader provides the top-down direction to innovate.

These leaders often take an active role in innovation, sometimes actually working on projects. They are adroit at spotting opportunities and elaborating on how to expand offerings such as tying services to products; they are extremely good at being team players and involve all the necessary stakeholders early in the life of a project; they are decisive and provide the will to cancel projects that do not meet expectations;

and they develop other peoples' ability to innovate by providing time, resources, and legitimacy for people to work on innovation projects.

In addition, Innovation Leaders create and care for the innovation structure and ensure all parties of the innovation effort in the company are chartered, functioning, resourced, and excited about what they are doing.

Innovation Portfolio Committee

Under the direction of the Innovation Leader (see Fig. 6-6), the IPC obtains resources from the rest of the organization and then charters and assembles Innovation Project Teams to manage each project.

The Committees are assigned to carry out the innovation function for breakthrough rather than incremental innovations. They incorporate a minimum amount of structure and resources while maintaining maximum flexibility to address a wide variety of innovation projects. Committee activities include stimulating and evaluating new ideas: acquiring funding, providing business coaching, planning for adoption, maintaining an innovation database, and commissioning and forming Innovation Project Teams.

To start an IPC, the company must make a number of decisions, including:

- **Decision Rights**: This should include decision-making responsibilities, roles, number of people, budget discretion, and whether all votes are equal.
- **Objectives**: Examples include top-line growth through market drivers utilizing marketing, IP, and R&D resources; providing opportunities for personnel to innovate; and strengthening the company's innovation culture.
- **Area of Representation**: These include science areas as well as other functions such as Production, Finance, R&D, and Marketing.
- **Governance**: The chair should report to senior management/Innovation Leader.
- **Membership**: The ideal is two or three long-term members and six to ten rotating members on a two- or three-year rotation. It is important to have respected experts.
- **Roles and Responsibility**: Innovators submit ideas. Committee members evaluate and provide coaching to innovators.

- **Budget**: Funding should be available for both internal and external work to demonstrate the potential of ideas.
- **Idea Management Activities**: How proactive will the Committee be in stimulating new projects, managing projects, providing connections, providing structured processes, and monitoring the spending?
- **Innovation Culture Activities**: From the beginning, the Committee needs to agree on the extent and type of cultural change to be attempted.
- **Startup Activities**: Determine launch activities and promote the Committee's activities, especially successful launches.

In addition to managing a portfolio of innovation projects, the IPC may also stimulate cultural change by engaging in such activities as:

- Creating innovation training
- Holding problem-solving workshops
- Offering an external speakers program
- Documenting and publicizing innovation
- Establishing networks and forums
- Initiating awards and recognition programs

Establishing an IPC typically begins with a two-day workshop for the people involved. The **Innovation Portfolio Committee Worksheet** features an agenda will help you cover all the necessary issues. Not every committee will engage in all activities, but you can choose the content depending on your organization's specific objectives. The Innovation Leader, in consultation with stakeholders and participants, should determine that content ahead of time.

Use the IPC Worksheet by selecting the elements of the committee's charter in the first column before the sessions begin. At the sessions, participants make specific decisions about how to implement each element. Specific actions are decided, and the people responsible are assigned.

IPCs should be structured with the flexibility to adapt to any variety of projects simultaneously. They need flexibility and autonomy to choose new lines of action that traditional resource-constrained and performance-driven operational units may not be able to support. By remaining associated with their home departments, Committee members are still able to help get opportunities adopted.

Innovation Portfolio Committee Worksheet		
IPC Creation Agenda	Decisions and Action Plans	Person Assigned and Date Completed
Startup Session 1: Idea Management		
Innovation Charter		
Codify founding decisions		
Committee roles and responsibilities		
Establish norms and ground rules		
Idea Management Processes		
Submission form and instructions		
Evaluation form and training materials		
Database management features		
Funding Decision Model		
Elaborate/plan		
Development		
Time frame		
Logistics		
Business Coaching		
Compelling case		
Adoption planning		
Adoption Planning		
Targets		
Trials		
Operational Tempo		
Anticipated pace of activities and results		
Start Up Session 2: Innovation Culture		
Stimulating Ideas		
Promotion plan		
Communication architecture		
Innovation Training		
For the Committee		
Innovation Management concepts		
Business Case Coaching		
For the idea submitters		

Innovation Portfolio Committee Worksheet
How to sell brilliant ideas
For the rest of the organization
External Speakers
Topics
People
Documenting Innovation
Newsletters, etc.
Communication Architecture
Networks and Forums
Community of practice
Meetings
Awards and Recognition
Past
Future

Every IPC will be different, even within the same company, depending on the innovation objectives of a specific unit. Nevertheless, we note some general management principles that can help maintain operational focus and facilitate relationships with the rest of the organization:

- Establish a specific and unique mechanism for considering and governing the portfolio of major innovation ventures. Ideally all projects should be compared against each other in a single portfolio view. This is easier to achieve with a centralized system.

- Use an options mentality for project evaluation, with an allowance for reconsideration of expired options. Establish a valuation process for project- and portfolio-level go/kill decisions.

- Install a mechanism for governing or overseeing each portfolio project composed of project-specific expertise. It is impossible for a single body to have the depth of understanding needed to guide all projects. Project-specific governance boards are needed and may evolve as projects advance.

- Establish a procedure for constant reflection and reconfiguration, which are essential for the Committee's long-term viability. High-flexibility organizations require organizational autonomy to reconfigure.

- Define and agree on roles and responsibilities. To consider: Hybrid reporting relationships often are needed. Subject matter experts continue to report to their respective VPs. Project teams report through innovation VP.

IPCs may charter Innovation Project Teams at any level of development they consider appropriate. For example, they may commission a team to start innovating in a particular strategic area, or, conversely, they may start a team only after an idea has been developed into an opportunity with a compelling case written. It depends on the strategic importance, timing, and level of risk the IPC wants.

A critical IPC function is to cancel projects. Projects must be both easy to start and easy to stop. Some organizations have a cultural norm that makes it difficult to end a project, even after they determine it won't work out. The IPC must establish and enforce project support and continuation criteria. We will have more to say about metrics in the next section.

Innovation Project Teams

Innovation Project Teams (IPT) often consist of the person who suggested the idea, along with other subject-matter experts from across the disciplines involved in the idea's development and deployment. IPTs are temporary and exist only for the work of a specific project. Their time commitment can vary from a few hours per month to full time. The team members are usually part-time until the project is less risky and further development decisions require full-time, dedicated personnel.

Switching to full-time management can be a troublesome transition for the team because the originator and/or champion may or may not have the skills and/or desire to continue with the project. The IPC must continuously monitor and counsel team members about the advisability of their continued participation. At the conclusion of a project, IPT members return to their usual tasks. We have observed that once a person has been through a real breakthrough project, their view of the business is forever changed.

Measure and Improve

As you can now tell, we view the System as much more than another New Product Development (NPD) process. We see it as a strategic process for companies that want to win and grow in their markets.

Ultimately, all differences between companies in price, function, or cost derive from the hundreds of activities required to create, produce, sell, and deliver their products and services: Namely, *how the company innovates and creates commercial value.* Differentiation arises from both the choice of activities and how they are performed. Hence, the innovation system is not some separate and distinct plan; for companies pursuing competitive advantage and growth, the innovation and production systems should be united.

To achieve the full benefit of the System, you must link it to your business strategy through performance metrics. We use the *Balanced Scorecard* tool by Kaplan and Norton as a systematic way to measure the System's impact on the company (5).

Balanced Scorecard

We create a *Balanced Scorecard* by bringing together existing and new worksheets. A typical *Balanced Scorecard* contains four types of metrics or perspectives:

1. Financial Outcomes: The *Breakeven Analysis* in Fig. 5-13 identifies the critical financial measures of upfront investment required, operating loss, time to profit, time to recover investment, and the size of the benefit in the long run. In the *Breakeven Analysis*, these measures are plotted on a time dimension that shows investors how the innovation is impacting the company financially.

2. Customer Outcomes: The **Buyer Utility Map** (see Chapter 5: *Module 2, Create the Compelling Case*) is used as a final summary of how customers benefit from the innovations.

3. Internal Business Processes: The System as a process itself is measured in the **Innovation Project Metrics Worksheet** and the **Innovation Process Metrics Worksheet**. These worksheets measure the System's activities by tracking:

- The number of ideas submitted
- The number of opportunities created
- The number of business cases accepted into NPD
- The System cycle time (the length of time from when the idea was first submitted until it is formally adopted into the NPD process)

4. Learning and Growth: The System uses CIMS' Innovation Management Maturity Assessment (IMMA) to measure your organization's ability to put the System for Industrial Innovation into effect and to institutionalize it. The IMMA measures the organizations proficiency in five competencies:

1. Idea Management
2. Market Management
3. Portfolio Management
4. Platform Management
5. Project Management

We construct a *Balanced Scorecard* by using existing and new tools described below.

Innovation Project Metrics Worksheet

The **Innovation Project Metrics Worksheet** provides critical progress information about each project. It follows the flow of the System, so each major step along the innovation path is represented. By assembling the worksheets already completed by following the System, you can easily obtain a comprehensive summary about each project.

Innovation Project Metrics Worksheet		
Metric	**Worksheet**	**Date Completed**
Idea Submitted	Idea Description Worksheet	
Business Opportunity	Opportunity Development Worksheet	
Business Case	Business Case Template	
Adoption	Decision-ready Checklist	
SII Cycle Time	# Days	

NOTE: OVERALL SII CYCLE TIME (MEASURED IN DAYS) = DATE OF IDEA SUBMITTED TO DATE OF ADOPTION

Innovation Process Metrics Worksheet

To get a program view of the impact the System is having on the organization, the IPC collects the **Innovation Project Metrics Worksheet** from each Innovation Project Team's project and summarizes the results using the **Innovation Process Metrics Worksheet.** This worksheet measures the Team's—and System's—overall ability to efficiently generate, select, develop, and launch new business opportunities.

SII (System for Industrial Innovation) Cycle Time (average) is the culmination of these efforts. It takes into account issues of leadership, skills availability, resource limitations, learning curve, training, and so forth. As we discussed in Chapter 3, *A System for Industrial Innovation*, one of the System's chief objectives is to provide organizations with a process that enables the transition of breakthrough ideas across the Valley of Death to commercialization—efficiently and effectively. As such, SII Cycle Time (average) makes an excellent chief metric to represent the Internal Business Process performance of the System

Innovation Process Metrics Worksheet	
Measure	**Metric** *Taken from Innovation Project Worksheets*
Number of Ideas Submitted	
Number of Business Opportunities Developed	
Number of Business Cases Approved	
Number of Business Opportunities Adopted	
SII Cycle Time Average _____	

The Innovation Management Maturity Assessment

To measure learning and growth within companies, CIMS offers the Innovation Management Maturity Assessment (IMMA). The IMMA is an easy-to-use, web-based tool for measuring an organization's ability to manage innovation. It is based on the CIMS Innovation Management Framework, which defines the specific innovation metrics critical for success.

Key Competencies

The IMMA identifies the five essential "competencies," or capabilities, leading organizations possess that enable them to recognize new opportunities, select appropriate ideas, and design and efficiently develop new and attractive solutions. These competencies are Idea Management, Market Management, Portfolio Management, Platform Management, and Project Management. The IMMA also tracks the maturation, or progression, of these competencies in your organization.

These five competencies have been referred to throughout the System. It should be noted that competencies are not processes, although there is a logical workflow from breakthrough ideas ultimately developing into high-impact commercial projects.

Management Dimensions

Each competency is divided into five dimensions: Strategy, Organization & Culture, Processes, Techniques & Tools, and Metrics. These management dimensions cross all competencies and represent the tools to build strong, durable, innovation management capabilities.

The competencies and dimensions create a heat map that can identify areas of strength and weakness and help decision makers prioritize innovation activities. Fig. 6-7 shows what a typical heat map of your organization's innovation capabilities might look like. In this example, there are weaknesses in the Competencies of Market and Platform Management and in the Dimensions of Organization & Culture and Metrics. These constitute innovation weak spots, which, in this case, include having a culture that fails to support marketing involvement in innovation. Please see Chapter 7, *Tools and Techniques*, for a more in-depth description of the IMMA.

IMMA Heat Map

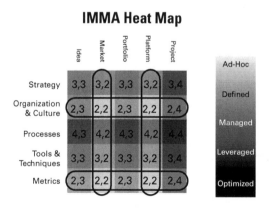

Figure 6-7. The IMMA heat map helps companies understand where their innovation maturity stands along a continuum.

Innovation Scorecard

Borrowing from the *Balanced Scorecard* (5), we pull innovation tools from the System to create an Innovation Scorecard. Together, the *Breakeven Analysis* (see Fig. 5-13), the **Buyer Utility Map Worksheet**, the **Innovation Program Metrics Worksheet**, and the *IMMA* (see Fig. 6-7) form a balanced method to measure breakthrough innovation in your company. As depicted in Fig. 6-8, these tools should be rendered together on a single page.

As users follow the System, the *Breakeven Analysis* and *Buyer Utility Map* are developed at the individual project level. Therefore, they should be summed to depict the full innovation portfolio. The **Innovation Process Metrics** and IMMA are already measured at the program level.

Innovation Scorecard

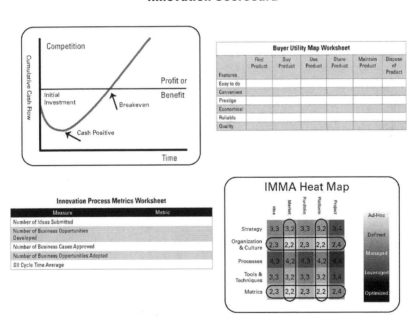

Figure 6-8. Several measurement tools come together to form the Innovation Scorecard.

Summing Up the System

At this point, if you have been completing the forms and worksheets, you should have a complete system for conducting breakthrough innovation. As we noted at the outset, breakthrough innovation requires a system because large-scale innovation will affect the entire organization. The use of a system demands complete involvement by every business group in order to create, evaluate, substantiate, and implement new ideas. Indeed, innovation must be system-wide.

The illustration below, which we have used throughout this book, represents such a system.

System for Innovation

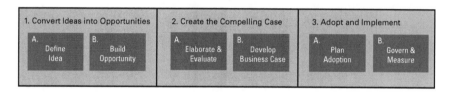

Figure 6-9. The System breaks the process into six manageable components.

In *Module 1: Convert Ideas into Opportunities*, ideas are defined and then converted into business opportunities if they meet two crucial conditions: (1) they are tied to enduring customer needs, and (2) the organization has the ability to deliver.

In *Module 2: Create the Compelling Case*, opportunities are elaborated upon, evaluated, and compared in a portfolio. Decisions are made to develop a compelling Business Case for selected opportunities.

In *Module 3: Adopt and Implement,* the chosen project Business Cases are prepared for adoption. The module concludes with the structure and tools for integrating the innovation effort into the permanent fabric of the organization, along with metrics for assessing the organization's innovation potential and the tools to manage innovation on an ongoing basis.

As we have shown, the System provides proven guidelines for conducting breakthrough innovation in capital-intensive, mature organizations operating in highly constrained environments. It includes specific, tested tools for assembling and applying the critical information you need to make strategic decisions. And it also includes the means to gather and analyze vast amounts of information through Big Data analytics, which we explain more fully in Chapter 7, *Tools and Techniques*.

REFERENCES FOR CHAPTER 6

1. O'Connor, G.C. 2008. "Major Innovation as a Dynamic Capability: A Systems Approach." *Journal of Product Innovation Management*, 25: 313-330.

2. Markham, S.K., and Lee, H. 2013. "Product Development and Management Association's 2012 Comparative Performance Assessment Study." *Journal of Product Innovation Management*, 30: 408-429.

3. Markham, S.K., and Lee, H. 2013. "Use of an Innovation Board to Integrate the Front End of Innovation with Formal NDP Processes: A Longitudinal Study." *Research-Technology Management*, 56: 37-44.

4. Mugge, P., and Markham, S.K. 2013. "An Innovation Management Framework." *The PDMA Handbook of New Product Development*, 35-50. John Wiley and Sons, Hoboken, New Jersey.

5. Kaplan, R.S., and Norton, D.P. 1992. "The *Balanced Scorecard*—Measures that Drive Performance." *Harvard Business Review,* 70: 71-79.

Notes:

CHAPTER 7.

Tools and Techniques

Introduction

In this chapter, we offer innovators a more in-depth discussion of the tools and techniques necessary for breakthrough innovation that were described in earlier chapters. These are:

- Using Big Data for industrial innovation. In this section, we explain the difference between the usual Big Data applications and the specialized way we approach Big Data to help make decisions around the implementation of breakthrough innovation.

- An 8-Step Process for using Big Data to answer the kind of unstructured questions you will have to address in the implementation process. This tool is a core capability for innovators because it uncovers previously unknowable information early enough in the idea development stage to make well-informed decisions when they matter most.

- A list of techniques typically used to find articulated customer needs.
- Commonly used techniques to find unarticulated customer needs.
- Commonly used techniques to find internal capabilities inside your organization.
- Commonly used techniques to find external capabilities outside your organization.
- A list of important readings in this area.

Big Data for Industrial Innovation

Previous chapters often noted that Big Data analytics is a powerful tool for innovation. Big Data analytics actually encompasses a wide variety of techniques that can be used for many applications. In this section, we describe the techniques we use at CIMS to help make critical decisions for breakthrough innovations.

Big Data is usually characterized as having a high volume of data, a high velocity of data, and a high variety of data. A fourth characteristic referring to the validity of the data is usually added: veracity (1). Some may successfully argue that existing data analytic techniques already address all four characteristics. In fact, large data sets using real-time operational data from a wide variety of inputs have been used for decades.

But what makes Big Data different is the way it is assembled. Programs such as Hadoop distribute the data-gathering tasks to multiple CPUs and allow access to the data through a master node or central CPU. In this way, Big Data can both gather and analyze orders of magnitude more data than other data-gathering techniques.

Making a Decision

To use Big Data to make an innovation decision, one must follow this procedure: (1) select the project, (2) state the question to be asked, (3) create a dictionary or list of the associated terms to search for, (4) build a decision model, (5) identify sources of information, (6) apply Big Data gathering techniques, (7) assess the data, and (8) make the decision.

Big Data's results are similar to what you get when searching Google: a list of references is created with your search words highlighted. These highlights are called "annotations." The annotations are the critical pieces of information you asked the computer to search for.

How you use the information depends on the question and criteria you set.

These steps will be covered in greater detail in the discussion on the 8-Step Process. Before learning how to use Big Data to make a decision, however, it is important to understand what we mean when we say Big Data and how we employ it to make decisions.

Structured and Unstructured Data

Another—and important—characteristic of Big Data is the degree to which we can use it to analyze unstructured text and identify what we seek among millions of documents. Unlike such commonly used search engines as Google, Big Data can search combinations of multiple lists of words simultaneously. For example, Google searches for two terms in a text based on their proximity and returns millions of documents based on an ever-widening dispersion of those words. This is why results following the first page or two are generally not helpful.

Big Data, in contrast, allows you to search for all associated words simultaneously. For example, if you are researching a specific company, you can look for all variants of the company name simultaneously, including different nomenclature such as the following designations for a company's organizing structure: Inc., INC, Incorporated, LLC, Llc., CO., Co., Company, Corporation, and so on. This method does not return millions of unrelated responses the way search engines do, but rather isolates a few critically relevant ones.

There are many solutions to analyzing data by putting numbers into rows and columns. These structured approaches often use operational data or market research data for questions you have specific hypotheses for. Although we do not avoid analyzing structured data, such reports generally tell us what happened in the past. When we want to know what might happen in the future, though, structured data becomes less useful. Unstructured data analyses, on the other hand, provide methods to find insights in written text. Unstructured data highlighting customer sentiment in social media, for example, can help predict market acceptance of a competitor's new product that resembles one your company is planning to launch. Opinions about new legislation or competitor moves are critical for strategic, rather than operational, decision making. Whereas structured data can be added, subtracted, multiplied, and divided, unstructured data can find statements about the likelihood of new legislation critical to your industry passing, just to name one example of the strategic value of unstructured text analytics.

Aggregation vs. Isolation

Another fundamental benefit of the techniques used to analyze unstructured data is that they allow us to isolate critical information rather than merely aggregate information. Aggregation techniques manipulate the data to expose patterns that identify problems, point out trends, or highlight areas of opportunity. Any time you add, subtract, multiply, or divide data or conduct statistical analysis on it, you are aggregating it. Isolation refers to finding a single specific piece of information that may not be subject to mathematical manipulation. For example, in assessing competitor actions, we might learn from a local newspaper that our chief rival is planning to open a distribution center in our market. If we had not taken advantage of unstructured data analytics, we might have had to wait until sales data revealed we had lost market share. Isolating such critical pieces of information is a powerful tool for making innovation decisions.

Another common Big Data question is how to find new customers for new and existing products. To find new customers, we identify characteristics of existing customers and then search for those characteristics among a larger group of companies by examining millions of documents. To find customers for products that don't exist yet, we look for people with the characteristics expressed in the Buyer Utility Map from Chapter 5, Module 2: *Create the Compelling Case*. In either case, you are looking for isolated chunks of information in order to identify a new customer.

For instance, a manufacturer of metal fabrication equipment wanted to know if their existing customers needed additional equipment. The equipment was expensive and required significant time to make. If the company waited until its customers requested said equipment, it would take too much time to manufacture, at which point the customer would likely go to a competitor. But building this equipment to inventory would be too expensive. The project team downloaded all financial information from all companies in the metals fabrication industry classification in the Securities and Exchange Commission (SEC) database to see which companies were increasing spending on manufacturing equipment.

Using unstructured text analytics, we then read all the newspapers in the U.S. to find articles announcing the building or expansion of manufacturing facilities. Then, we searched for all building permits in the country to find which of those companies had filed with local authorities to build new facilities. What resulted was a list of companies that were increasing their equipment budget, building or expanding facilities, and adding new employees (including how many hires were projected). The list also provided the size of the new facilities and the types of products that would be built in the new plants, projected one year or more into the future. This valuable information allowed the manufacturer to approach its potential customers in time to sell the equipment and manufacture it for on-time delivery.

Types of Innovation Information

Big Data can be used to find information that will answer a variety of other innovation questions. Below is a list of actual questions from among dozens of innovation projects CIMS has taken on using Big Data analytics.

- **Ask Simple Questions**: A clinical research organization wants to know what companies are conducting multiple myeloma trials, how successful they have been, and what the reasons for failure are.

- **Test a Hypothesis**: An employment-services company wants to confirm that its new staffing model will reduce turnover.

- **Assess Strategic Direction**: A bulk-chemical company wants to know whether it should enter into a certain branded-market space.

- **Find a Customer**: An industrial gas company wants to find new customers for its product among existing contacts and new market spaces.

- **Find a New Market or Use**: A consumer products company wants to find new uses for a mature product.

- **Gather Business Intelligence**: A packaging company wants to monitor customer, competitor, and legislative sentiment.

The example below gives descriptive information found for a clinical research organization.

Q & A: Example of Descriptive Information and Information Found

Q. Which companies and institutions are conducting multiple myeloma clinical trials?	A. 21 companies conducting 1249 trials in 54 sites
Q. Who are the industry leaders and investigators involved?	A. Identified the managers of seven of these projects
Q. How many clinical trials have failed and why	A. 91% were terminated or withdrawn due to lack of enrollment, 5% due to lack of compound, and 4% for undisclosed or other reasons
Q. What pharmacological products are currently being tested and which biochemical pathways are being targeted?	A. Identified the 20 gene targets being used by these 21 companies
Q. Are any companies working with these compounds or targeting these biochemical pathways, but not investigating multiple myeloma?	A. Identified 7 companies using these same gene targets for indications such as asthma, breast and lung cancer, Parkinson's, Alzheimer's, sickle cell anemia, blindness

Figure 7-1. Big Data helped this drug company find answers to its critical questions.

Big Data Decision Models

The decision model is central to using Big Data for innovation. The model is the set of thinking exercises for identifying critical information needs, sources of information, and the causal relationships between different pieces of information. Unstructured text analytics is ideal for identifying crucial questions, one of which might involve deciding if existing customers are logical prospects for your new product.

For example, in the case of an industrial gas supplier, you could start by downloading SEC financial data for every company on your customer list. Then look for structured information such as new R&D investments and unstructured information such as SEC disclosures and press releases from related equipment suppliers to see which customer is buying new equipment that uses the supplier's gases. This allows you to model how the industry works, which variables can be found in which sources, and how those variables relate to each other.

Models come in astonishing variety and are easily customized to your specific question. You do not need to be a high-level programmer or statistician to use unstructured text analysis; most market researchers, product developers, and operational people can use the modern text analytic tools. What is essential, however, is that users employ critical thinking to establish the proper context for searching for information and understanding the results. Although statisticians and computer programs can sometimes be good at this, we find that business decision makers are more adept at building critical and useful models for making business decisions.

Not Information Technology

Big Data analytics relies on information technology, but it is *not* an IT tool. Like other programs such as email or word processing, it is simply a platform that your IT department will need to support. Your business analysts will use it to gather and feed information into your decision-making process.

How Big Data Analytics Works

Big Data must apply the expertise of your subject-matter specialists to develop a search model. A model consists of categories of related terms and the relationship among those terms. A model tells the computer what to search for; it is the logic that identifies the important information you request. Big Data then applies that model to gather information from tens of millions of sources, applying the exact same criteria to every document search.

We use Natural Language Processing (NLP) to apply the model to unstructured text. This allows the computer to "understand" what you are looking for. For example, if you are seeking customer reaction to your product, you can distinguish sarcasm from compliments and insults. You can also use NLP to understand slang and regional idioms.

The major benefit of Big Data is that it collects data from multiple sources at the same time. Hadoop is an open-source program virtually every Big Data company uses to gather data. Hadoop distributes the task of gathering information among many computers and then combines the information into a single file. Because Big Data collects both structured and unstructured data, a wide variety of information can be assembled using Hadoop. Furthermore, MapReduce, a programming paradigm developed by Google, allows for easier organization of large data sets (2).

When Hadoop and MapReduce are used in unison, it creates an efficient analysis method for large datasets such as Big Data. Once the data is gathered, any appropriate method can be used to render an analysis.

Natural Language Processing is just one way to use the data Hadoop assembles. You can also use Hadoop to gather transactional or operational data and create structured data sets in real time. In the structured data case, the data are sent to a data analytics or statistics program such as SAS, R, or SPSS. Analyses and visual renderings are created to aid decision making. By establishing decision rules such as, "Reorder more inventory when the inventory reaches a certain point or sales velocity increases by X percent," you can rely on structured data to help with these types of decisions, but these are usually operational rather than strategic.

Structure of the Big Data Market

Big Data is as much a market structure as a technology. The Big Data market has three levels:

- Level 1 involves the hardware and software vendors that provide the actual equipment for conducting Big Data analytics (including IBM, SAS, SAP, Apache, Oracle, SQL Server, and Sybase).

- Level 2 encompasses the infrastructure providers that adapt hardware and software capabilities for Big Data use. These companies put the computations, storage, Internet access, and visualization tools together. Examples include Amazon, Infochimps, Google BigQuery, Teradata, Marklogic, SAS, Alteryx, and Cognos.

- Level 3 includes companies that use Big Data to do something: optimize operations, increase sales, make innovation decisions, conduct market research, conduct business intelligence studies, and more. These include Metamarkets, Media Science, Splunk, Predictive Policing, BloomReach, Blue Fin, and Data Decision Models.

These are just a few examples; there are many more companies in each of these levels, often working in multiple levels.

What It Takes To Do Big Data Analytics

Hardware

Although specialized equipment can increase performance, off-the-shelf components will get you started. A couple of pointers:

- Access to the Internet is critical. Most companies already have adequate bandwidth for Big Data demonstrations. For moderate-sized projects using one to 10 terabytes of data, it may take a few days to complete a crawl for your desired data.
- Multiple terabyte size storage is needed. The advantage of Big Data is that it uses your decision model to check hundreds of millions of documents. Doing this will require tens of terabytes of storage.

Software

All of the software components listed below are available as open source. However, proprietary software may provide more support. We've included one open source and one or two proprietary programs that we think are best in class in each category.

- Hadoop to process information
- A web crawler to find information on the Internet or on a company's Intranet (Nutch, Big Sheets)
- A database (Mongo, SQL)
- A natural language processor (GATE, IBM Content Analytics)
- A statistical analysis package (R, SAS, SPSS)

Skills

Most of the skills are already generally available. However, the managerial ability to integrate the interdisciplinary perspectives of different subject-matter experts to model decisions in unstructured text is a specialized skill. As mentioned before, high-level program and statistical tools are not necessary. Here are six common skills needed to perform Big Data analytics in a corporate environment:

- IT administration to make sure everything is working
- Programming
- Decision modeling

- Visualization
- Business and technical subject-matter expertise
- Decision making

A Decision Modeler

Decision modeling is the most critical task in using Big Data and unstructured text. The decision modeler must be skilled in using the hardware and software as well as decision models; he or she must also be able to manage individual subject-matter experts. The modeler should be an experienced and computer savvy business leader adept at integrating interdisciplinary inputs.

In addition, decision modelers should be able to:

- Use Internet crawlers to gather vast amounts of targeted information.
- Conduct a map-reduction process to create a data file from the raw information.
- Help subject-matter experts form meaningful questions about a specific problem or question.
- Formulate decision criteria.
- Identify pertinent sources of data.
- Classify problems and questions.
- Build specialized dictionaries of terms.
- Design rules that pinpoint specific pieces of information.
- Present and explain unstructured text results to management.
- Apply Big Data to the strategy of the decision makers.

Most important, even though the decision modeler may employ sophisticated software, he or she must be an incisive and critical thinker, able to frame the problem in meaningful terms and create the necessary structure to understand unstructured information.

In short, Big Data components are readily available, making Big Data analytics for innovation practical today. But it requires expertise to be able to use Big Data profitably. Just buying the equipment, including the analytical skills, is only useful when managers have the critical thinking skills to apply the Big Data capability. This is why the System and Big Data tools must be used together.

The 8-Step Process for Making Innovation Decisions with Big Data

We present the 8-Step Process as a series of steps with formatted worksheets to help users gather information for using Big Data to make innovation decisions. The worksheets should not be filled out until you have modified them to meet the information requirements of your particular project. The information in the worksheets—even the rows and columns that provide direction for what information to gather—should be considered examples only.

The 8-Step process can be used to answer a single stand-alone question. In this case, you do not need to use the System at all. You simply employ the 8-Step process to guide you through answering a specific question.

As presented here, you can also use the 8-Step process in conjunction with the System. There are numerous places in the System where the 8-Step Process can be used when other tools and techniques, like conventional market research tools, fail to satisfy your project's information requirements.

Step 1: Select and Identify Project

The 8-Step process begins by assembling a team of subject-matter experts who have both the technical and business acumen to ask pertinent questions, establish criteria, identify search terms and sources of information, specify the causal relationships between variables, and, finally, evaluate results in relationship to the original question. The team will reconvene after the search has been conducted to evaluate the data that's been extracted and answer the questions posed in Step 1.

Select and Identify Project Worksheet (Step 1)		
Indicate which step and sub-step in the System you are in	Question: State the question(s) you have about the step you are in	Criteria: For the step and question you are in state your criteria
Idea x	Is there an enduring customer need for high-efficiency smart-phone batteries?	Strategic Fit: *NA*
Opportunity		Market Demand: *Size and Growth Rate*
Elaborate		Supply Availability: *NA*
Evaluate		Competition: *NA*
Business Case		Business Environment: *NA*
Measure		Financial Opportunity: *Price and cost*

The first column in the **Select and Identify Project Worksheet** asks you to pinpoint where in the larger System you still need information. It then asks you what question or inquiry you wish to make and, following that, to identify the criteria for making a decision around the answer. For example, if you are examining the possibility of investing in high-efficiency smart-phone-battery manufacturing, you would establish criteria for market size and growth rate, and possibly price and cost trends, in order to confirm an enduring customer need.

Step 2: Formulate the Question

Formulate a question you need answered and then identify the topics or subjects in that question. For example, your question might include the topics of "high efficiency" and "batteries." We recommend you pose one question at a time since the answer to one question often leads to many other questions.

Formulate the Question Worksheet (Step 2)	
State your question from Step 1. Indicate topics in the question (bold and underline). For example: Will product A be viable in market B?	Is there an enduring customer **need** for **high-efficiency smart-phone batteries?**

Step 3: Create the Dictionary

For each topic in your question, create a list of terms that will help you search for information. These lists are often called dictionaries. Each topic in the question becomes a column heading to develop a list of terms and phrases—the dictionary—that relates to each topic of the question.

Create Dictionary Worksheet (Step 3)		
Dictionary 1: **Need**	Dictionary 2: **High-efficiency batteries**	Dictionary 3: **Smart-phone batteries**
Need	Discharge capacity	Handheld batteries
Demand	Power density	Cell-phone batteries
Want	Self-discharge	Power cells
Require	Fast recharge	

Step 4: Create Decision Rules

Rules are logical statements that help you search for the information necessary to answer your questions. Crossing two or more dictionaries to find results of intersecting terms is one way to create a rule. For example, if your question is to learn whether or not there is a need for high-efficiency smart-phone batteries, you will have a list of terms for "high-efficiency batteries" and "smart-phone batteries." When you combine both lists into a rule, the resulting information that is annotated or highlighted will contain both "high-efficiency batteries" and "smart-phone batteries" terms together. Note that rule creation is executed on dictionaries. This means that results will be found or returned for any of the terms in the dictionaries, not just the name of the dictionary. If you add a dictionary of need terms you will get results that contain information related to the needs for high-efficiency smart-phone batteries.

The crossing of all three dictionaries is an example of a rule (see **Create Decision Rules Worksheet**).

Crossing dictionaries to create rules is deceptively simple. But it is essential that you understand the outcomes of the rules. The outcomes or annotations are the results. Since the results can contain a combination of any terms from the dictionaries, it is important to know what you are looking for in the results. Therefore, for each rule you should state what you expect to find from that rule.

Create Decision Rules Worksheet (Step 4)	
Rules (dictionary combinations)	Expected outcomes
Smart-phone batteries X high-efficiency batteries	Information about high-efficiency smart-phone batteries
High-efficiency batteries X need	Information about the need for high-efficiency batteries (all high-efficiency batteries—not just for smart phones)
Need X smart-phone batteries X high-efficiency batteries	Information about the need for high-efficiency smart-phone batteries

Step 5: Information Sources

Identify sources of information that are relevant to your question. For example, if you want to know about technical advances in high-efficiency batteries, search academic and government sources of technical information rather than social media. On the other hand, if you want to know whether customers prefer longer talk time as a smart phone feature, you could search social media blogs for comments and complaints. You may need different sources for each topic or dictionary.

Information Sources Worksheet (For Each Dictionary) (Step 5)		
Need	High-Efficiency Batteries	Smart-Phone Batteries
Product-oriented blogs	Government lab reports	Product brochures
Popular press product reviews	Scientific journals	Company announcements
Customer complaint logs	Company press releases	Industry publications
Conferences	Conference proceedings	

The reasoning and expected outcomes of the combination of dictionaries, rules, and sources constitute the decision model. This provides you with the information to answer your original questions.

Step 6: Gather Information

Most market researchers, product developers, and similarly trained professionals can learn to gather and analyze the data. Although it involves significant time and learning how to use a suite of specialized software, it does not require specialized statistical or programming skills. A modicum of experience, coupled with the ability to think critically as well as being informed about the content of the business decision, is critical. Nevertheless, following this process will help people develop the necessary skills.

The information obtained from Steps 1-5 provides the information necessary to perform a crawl to gather the data and tag all the terms. The result will be a list of annotated texts with their references. This display will resemble a Google search result except that the results will be based on dictionaries rather than single terms and your search terms will be highlighted.

You should involve the original group of content experts to identify the pertinent information. As they inspect the highlighted text, they will identify information that is related to each of the criteria identified in Step 1. It is critical at this step to identify and capture information for the question you are asking. The team can capture that information by simply copying and pasting it from the results file into the **Gather Information Worksheet.**

Gather Information Worksheet (Step 6)		
Criteria (from Step 1)	Confirming Information	Disconfirming Information

Step 7: Evaluate and Score Data

As the experts inspect the annotated results from Step 6, they cut and paste all the confirming and disconfirming information found into the appropriate column in the **Evaluate and Score Data Worksheet**. The information is then evaluated in terms of its ability to answer the question accurately enough for making an informed decision. Score that information on a 0 to 5 scale for how well it supports the original question on each of the criteria copied from Step 1 (0=no support, 5=strong support).

Evaluate and Score Data Worksheet (Step 7)					
Criteria (from Step 1)	Confirming and disconfirming information copied from the annotated text. (This will include extensive information).	Is the data sufficient to make an informed decision?			Score the data: 0= data does not support question 5=data clearly supports question
		Is there enough data?	Origin of the data	Is the data relevant?	
Strategic Fit	(information copied from annotations)	Yes	Social Media	Highly	5
Market Demand					
Supply Availability					
Competition					
Business Environment					
Financial Opportunity					

Chart the Results

Finish Step 7 by charting the results. Use a spider diagram or similar method to depict the scores visually. We find that the simpler the visualization, the better. The point is to grasp vast amounts of data in a single glance.

Spider Diagram Example

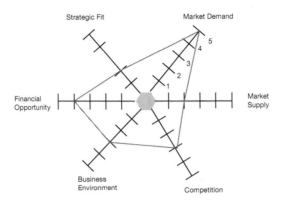

Figure 7-2. Spider diagrams enable readers to absorb vast amounts of data quickly.

Step 8: Make Decision

Start making the decision about your project by reconvening the same team of experts that carried out Step 1. These subject-matter experts should review the results, score the data, and make the final decision. They need to restate the original question and answer it with the supporting and non-supporting information; they should also indicate how the answer affects the rest of the project. For example, if the answer to your question is that there is no customer need for higher-efficiency smart-phone batteries, then you may want to kill the entire innovation project. The experts should note what the implications are for the answer and what action or actions should be taken as a result. If, for instance, they feel competitors and technologies are rapidly advancing, they might still recommend allocating more resources to develop high-efficiency batteries. The experts should also identify potential consequences of taking the course of action—such as falling behind competitors—as well as how much effort it would take to get ahead. Last, the group should make a final decision, in this case to pursue new high-efficiency battery manufacturing technologies—or not.

Make Decision Worksheet (Step 8)	
Original question	Is there an enduring customer need for high-efficiency smart-phone batteries?
Answer the original question?	Yes. (This answer is usually surrounded by qualifiers such as for certain segments of price ranges.)
How does this answer affect the rest of the information in the System for Industrial Innovation?	
What are the implications of the answer to the question?	
What course of action is implied by the answer to the question?	
What are the consequences of taking the action?	
What are the resource requirements if action is taken?	
State your final decision.	

Tips For Using the 8-Step Process

While the process is easy to follow, you can get more out of it by bearing in mind the following:

- It is an iterative process. Don't expect perfect results the first time.
- You will need to modify the terms in your dictionary.
- Your rules will need to be modified as you explore the data.
- You should ensure your model is working on a small test data set before using on a Big Data set.
- Check your results against a known quantity.
- Discuss the model with subject matter experts.
- Involve subject matter experts to evaluate and score the information and then make the decision—hopefully with more confidence.

Tools and Techniques Explained

In order for the System to work as designed, companies need to have accurate, detailed information about their customers' needs and their organizations' capabilities. What follows is an in-depth discussion of effective tools and techniques—briefly mentioned in earlier chapters—that can help you obtain this information.

Articulated Needs Search Techniques

Here are some proven techniques to help determine articulated customer needs.

• **Direct Inquiry.** Knowledgeable respondents are interviewed with prepared questions.

> **Technique**: Proper technique includes setting enough time to cover the intended topics in an environment conducive to in-depth discussion. Pre-written questions stimulate follow-on inquiries. Interviews usually go better with two interviewers who share the roles of questioner and recorder.
>
> **Advantages**: A simple technique for quickly eliciting in-depth information as well as follow-up comments with additional questions and explanations. Particularly useful at the start of a project when little is known about the area of inquiry.
>
> **Disadvantages**: Individual respondents may not be representative of the target population. Can take a long time and cost a lot to gather information from multiple respondents.
>
> **Requirements**: Quality results depend on selecting knowledgeable respondents, allowing sufficient time, preparing informed questions, and consolidating replies into reportable format.

• **Delphi Technique.** A common set of questions is sent to a group of informed respondents.

> **Technique:** A moderator prepares the questions for respondents, who answer them in isolation from other participants. The moderator combines the different answers and distributes them back to the respondents until they converge on answers or the different positions become clear. Respondents never meet or talk to one another directly.
>
> **Advantages:** Relatively fast and simple. Different points of view are treated equally so all opinions are registered. There is less posturing and face-saving behavior. Particularly good for gathering information and opinions and making potentially

contentious decisions. Can be done asynchronously through email. Easy for people to participate.

Disadvantages: Respondents cannot ask one another questions or build on their comments. Although it includes more than one person, the ability to generalize is still limited. Cannot be certain how thoughtfully participants answer questions. Cannot modify questions easily. Respondents may not understand one another.

Requirements: Moderator must be knowledgeable about the topic and familiar with applying the technique. The questions must be carefully prepared, and participants must be chosen with care.

• **Nominal Group Technique**. A knowledgeable group shares opinions in a sequential, structured process.

Technique: The moderator poses questions to the group, with each participant replying orally. Other participants cannot discuss the response but only ask clarifying questions. The same question is asked again until responses converge or positions become clear. The next question is then posed to the group. The group does not engage in open dialogue about one another's responses or ideas; they only present their own responses.

Advantages: The group interacts on a controlled basis that ensures mutual understanding and building on ideas. All opinions are given equal weight, preventing one or two people from monopolizing the time or the group going off on tangents. Particularly good at finding solutions to problems, considering different approaches, and converging on solutions. The group can modify questions and answers in real time.

Disadvantages: Participants cannot openly discuss or build on ideas individually, which limits the ability to make generalizations. Social interactions, status, and personalities may detract from objective analysis. It takes more time, may be difficult to schedule, and participants are constrained in topics they can bring up.

Requirements: Skilled facilitator. Discipline to execute the technique. Careful formulation of question. Selection of the right participants. Preparation of opening questions ahead of time.

• **Group Discussion**. A commonly used—and misused—technique to explore an issue.

Technique: A meeting sponsor assembles a representative group to discuss an issue. The group is given specific questions or problems to consider; it picks the facilitator or group leader, scribe, and process facilitator; and it considers the question and responds to the sponsor (for example, How do we reduce the cost of manufacturing?). The group often reports back to the sponsor in writing. A variety of sub-techniques can be used for group discussions, including sorting and categorizing techniques such as writing ideas on Post-it® notes. People with diverse backgrounds can be very effective at challenging existing conceptions and proposals.

Advantages: The group can explore complex issues, clarify and restate the questions, build on suggestions and ideas, and enjoy the experience more than with Delphi or nominal group techniques.

Disadvantages: Degrades into an unstructured conversation if not conducted properly. Group may diverge from the stated questions, and individuals may monopolize the discussion and bias the result. Discussions can be time consuming and difficult to schedule. Aggressive personalities can bias results, and personal rank in the organization can affect the participation and contributions of other participants.

Requirements: Suitable meeting place and sufficient time commitments from all participants. Questions and participants must be carefully selected to fit the issue being discussed. Group members must have the ability to work in these kinds of groups.

• **Discussion Prompts**. Assembled groups are given a prompt as a means of generating different solutions or opportunities.

Technique: Meeting objective is set ahead of time. A diverse group representing the range of people affected by the chosen topic meets. The facilitator presents the objective of the meeting along with a prompt. Prompts are ways of looking at the issue from a specific point of view or set of constraints (for instance, increase battery-power density by 50 percent in two years). The facilitator and/or group members take the roles of scribe, leader, and process monitor.

Advantages: Particularly good at bringing fresh perspectives to problems. Can reflect multiple points of view and resolve conflicting opinions and objectives. Good at providing a broad perspective on the needs associated with an issue. Can be very creative.

Disadvantages: More diverse than other group techniques, but it still might not be representative of the target demographic. Groups might not have the necessary expertise to identify real problems/needs, and the approaches they recommend may not be practical. Discussion may not relate to the primary purpose of the meeting.

Requirements: Skilled facilitator able to start, monitor, and control an open-ended and possibly high-energy discussion. Facilitator must choose an appropriate prompt that has an underlying analogy to the issues being addressed. Access to all the people affected by the issue.

• **Brainstorming.** A structured process to generate multiple alternatives to a single issue and then to assess and prioritize the options.

Technique: A diverse group of people are gathered, given an issue, and asked to think of as many ideas as possible. A person acting as scribe records all ideas in view of the other participants. As many ideas as possible are generated, no matter how improbable. No judgment or evaluation of ideas is allowed at this stage. When the group has exhausted all possibilities, the ideas are evaluated and ranked. Prompts may be given to help generate more ideas. Ideas may be written on Post-it® notes and categorized. The group then sets criteria and reviews the ideas and prioritizes.

Advantages: Develops and assesses a large number of options to address an issue. Particularly good for developing new ideas. Can be modified in numerous ways to address different issues, such as reverse brainstorming (how to cause the problem) used for problem solving.

Disadvantages: This common technique often degrades into an unstructured discussion. Ideas may not be useful; group dynamics, personality, and status may bias the outcomes.

Requirements: A clear objective to address. Willing participants familiar with the technique. A skilled facilitator to present the issue, encourage equal participation, and move the group through the different stages at the appropriate time.

Unarticulated Needs Search Techniques

Here are some proven techniques to help determine unarticulated customer needs.

• **Elaboration**. Existing internal or external innovation capabilities are presented to intended users to see if they recognize a use for them. These capabilities represent either existing company strengths or potential investments in new capabilities.

> **Technique**: Elaboration is a structured process in which a given set of company capabilities is systematically applied to create a new product or service. Possibilities are checked with users for degree of acceptance and need.

> **Advantages**: Elaboration can increase the quality of the original idea. It can also leverage innovation from one area to another, thereby reducing cost and time.

> **Disadvantages**: Elaboration can be time consuming and may cause the group to lose focus on its primary goals.

> **Requirements**: A broad group of knowledgeable people who can speak for the product and service needs of different intended user groups. Also requires skilled leader to run idea sessions.

• **Strategy/Portfolio Review**. A structured process where unarticulated needs are identified by examining the existing set of ideas and possible gaps in the project portfolio. Places in the portfolio without products could represent unarticulated needs.

> **Technique**: The existing strategy and/or portfolio is examined for places that are under-represented relative to the company's business strategy. These spaces represent strategic needs or places that lack ideas and solutions that must be found.

> **Advantages**: Focuses on projects that meet critical needs. Makes efficient use of resources because everyone knows what is being worked on, reducing duplication of efforts. Fastest way to achieve technical objectives. Allows more innovative projects to flourish.

> **Disadvantages**: Reduces participation of individual contributors.

> **Requirements**: A portfolio process that includes project selection, portfolio review tools, governance, metrics, and the managerial and staff skills and discipline to implement and maintain the portfolio.

• **Document or Library Search**. A process that identifies and systematically searches for internal and external documents related to the technology strategy. Comparing company activities with available solutions, emerging technologies, or practices at other companies identifies needs and ideas.

> **Technique:** Identify resources to access and search multiple databases that store information about both previous and ongoing technology development.

> **Advantages**: This technique can be fast and inexpensive. It also helps identify who has expertise in particular technologies, markets, or business analysis.

> **Disadvantages:** The databases may not include all of the records in any particular field. The company's own records might not reflect the industry state of the art. These searches can result in a very large output that requires refinement.

> **Requirements**: List of keywords or phrases to include or exclude in order to narrow search and reduce output. May need external help to search output for salient points.

• **Unstructured Text Analysis**. A computer-based method to read large amounts of unstructured text, such as web pages, and look for conversation threads that reveal previously unarticulated needs.

> **Technique:** Use a natural language interpretation method to scan large amounts of online text for technical opportunities. Employ content experts and people skilled in text analytics to develop search parameters.

> **Advantages**: Ability to review vast amounts of data with a single set of search parameters. Can search globally in multiple languages.

> **Disadvantages:** Can take significant expert time to develop effective search criteria. May produce a set of results that is too large to manage and implement efficiently.

> **Requirements**: Requires a person trained in setting up sophisticated searches. Also requires time from content experts to help define search parameters.

• **Early-Stage User Review**. Researchers determine how and where to observe key users solving related problems at the earliest stages of opportunity development.

Technique: Observation may take the form of simply watching, working alongside people, examining workflows, reading documentation, or even interviewing individuals or groups.

Advantages: Users are not always aware of their own needs; people taught a certain way to do things may be unaware of possible improvements. Therefore, asking them will yield little, although observation of a particular operation can reveal large opportunities for improvement. You may be able to see what people who are doing the actual work cannot see.

Disadvantages: People being observed do not act the same way they do when they're alone.

Requirements: Must observe people unobtrusively or over a long enough period that they get accustomed to the observer's presence. The observer must be open to many possible improvement opportunities.

• **Voice of the Customer (VOC).** This technique is used in an interview format to understand unarticulated needs of users/customers at an early stage. It helps to turn what users might say into addressable needs. VOC is not used to check ideas with customers but to understand their needs.

Technique: A VOC is conducted in four sequential steps:

1. Set the context by asking people about a specific experience.

2. Ask people to relate a story about their experience in a related domain area.

3. Ask specific probing questions about the details of the story.

4. Ask general questions about why they did what they did, the importance of it, how well things worked, and how they felt about the experience.

Advantages: Allows gathering a lot of detailed information about underlying needs.

Disadvantages: May not be generalizable beyond the one person. Will not produce workflow-type information (observation does that). It relies on the insight of the questioner to devise penetrating questions and recognize important insights.

Requirements: Ability to put the interviewee into a specific situation, develop specific probing questions ahead of time, ask appropriate general questions during the interview. Need to interview a number of people to avoid biasing results.

• **Lead-User Research**. Work with your lead or most advanced users to understand how they identify and solve problems.

> **Technique:** Identify customers or users who make the earliest or most advanced use of a technology, process, or system. Interview them or observe how they make use of the existing products in order to learn how they might need a new product or integrate existing solutions into meeting their needs. These lead users often provide opportunities for further development.

> **Advantages:** Products that come from lead users represent real market solutions rather than hypothetical solutions to assumed problems. An initial user class or customer set is described by the behavior and needs of the lead users. Yields high-quality data and solutions.

> **Disadvantages:** Can be costly and time consuming. Products can require extensive adaptation by the company. Integration of an externally derived solution may not be acceptable to the existing company.

> **Requirements**: Can be done with internal personnel, but is often conducted by external firms, which can be costly. The unit conducting the lead-user research must be involved in all phases of the research to ensure that the needs of the user remain the focus of the project. (Eric Von Hippel at MIT pioneered this technique and offers training, consulting, books, and other materials.)

• **Technology Scouting.** A systematic method for discovering new technologies as well as assessing their capabilities in order to gain insight into the needs they address.

> **Technique**: Emphasis is on finding long-term sources of technical development capabilities that could be useful to the company. Technology scouting can either be focused on a specific area or be more wide ranging. It requires a lateral-thinking generalist assigned full or part time on a permanent basis.

> **Advantages**: Can find developments before they are completed or known more widely. Advanced information on new technologies can facilitate quick, high-quality decisions about

the use of new technologies. Provides a deep, long-term view of development technical areas.

Disadvantages: May require long-term investment with uncertain results and is, therefore, difficult to justify financially.

Requirements: Assignment of a lateral thinker for a long period of time.

• **Environmental Scanning.** This is a method for looking at the macro environment.

> **Technique**: This involves identifying categories of variables to track on a permanent basis, although it can be done on a one-time basis. The category name forms the acronym PESTEL, which stands for Political, Economic, Social, Technological, Environmental, and Legal. These categories help the company assess markets, industries, governments, and so forth from a macro level and translate these trends onto the micro level such as customers, competitors, market segments, and regulations.

> **Advantages**: Provides a systematic way to assess what is happening outside the company in a defined area of inquiry. It can spot a break in a trend, which can be important to the company. It is very good for entering or refreshing a specific area of inquiry in order to get many people up to speed and working together.

> **Disadvantages**: It can be costly and time consuming to constantly monitor areas that may appear stable and yet be important. Information may be gathered but then not acted upon. It may be difficult to attract the relevant manager's attention and make important decisions based on the routine gathering of data.

> **Requirements**: Must have one or more people assigned on a permanent basis with specific training for conducting a PESTEL analysis. If done as a one-time activity, it may require considerable management and staff time.

• **PESTEL Analysis.** Assesses trends in order to identify capabilities the company needs to develop in order to maintain its competitive advantage.

> **Technique**: Collect information from a defined area of interest in order to spot patterns and trends. This may be done internally or externally and include PESTEL information: Political,

Economic, Social, Technological, Environmental, Legal. New trends can reveal new, needed capabilities for the company to develop.

Advantages: Addresses a wide variety of information. Helps avoid blind spots and costly mistakes resulting from looking at a problem too narrowly. As a forward-looking technique, it can spot important opportunities and threats long before other techniques.

Disadvantages: May require large amounts of effort without revealing anything new or important to the company.

Requirements: Must define area of focus and amount of effort properly to ensure meaningful results without wasting effort. Need people experienced with PESTEL analysis to facilitate the process.

• **Open Innovation.** A set of techniques for matching internal needs to external capabilities. Can also be used to identify needs that are being addressed externally as well as internal needs that are not being met.

Technique: A variety of tools and techniques that people inside the company can use proactively to search external sources of innovation for solutions to internal needs.

Advantages: Uses established innovation capabilities to search for and integrate a much larger set of sources and capabilities than possible inside the company.

Disadvantages: Can result in the generation of great effort for limited results. People inside the company may not accept ideas brought in from the outside. Search parameters may not be appropriate for what is needed.

Requirements: Define the scope of external searching carefully. Find internal or external resources and suppliers and commit to what can sometimes be an expensive activity.

Internal Capabilities Search Techniques

Here are some proven search techniques for finding capabilities within your company.

• **Interview Experts**. Going straight to an authoritative source can be very beneficial.

Technique: Identify likely experts to interview. Book enough time to cover the intended materials in a setting conducive to in-depth explanations and ask prepared questions that encourage follow-on inquiries. Interviews usually include two interviewers who share the roles of questioner and recorder.

Advantages: Simple means of eliciting in-depth information. Ability to follow up on comments with additional questions and explanations. Particularly useful at the start of a project when little is known about it.

Disadvantages: Single respondent may not be representative of the population of interest. Sometimes takes a long time to gather information.

Requirements: Quality results depend on selecting knowledgeable respondents, getting quality time, preparing informed questions, and consolidating the results into a reportable format.

• **Consult on Needs with Outside Communities of Practice or Other Networks**. This is a good way to broaden the scope of your knowledge.

Technique: Identify likely communities of practice in large organizations or other internal networks. Contact community leaders and learn the best way to approach their community. Identify individuals or subsets of people to contact. The leader may recommend addressing the full community in a specified forum such as a presentation or via email or newsletter. The point is to solicit useful methods from multiple experts.

Advantages: Connect with experts inside your company and if needed supplement with external experts. Multiple perspectives allow considering a broader set of possibilities. Also allows for a dialogue to assess proper fit of idea, expand on the idea, and assess its fit with multiple experts in the field.

Disadvantages: Access to experts may be difficult. Experts may be focused on an area tangential to the question. The idea may be new and outside the expertise of people inside your organization whose opinions might be mistaken as expert.

Requirements: Access to communities of practice and other R&D groups. Need to prepare carefully constructed questions and follow-up questions to gather opinions efficiently and effectively.

• **Document or Library Search**. Identifies and systematically searches for internal and external documents related to technology solutions.

> **Technique**: Identify resources to access, such as government databases, and search multiple databases that store information about previous and ongoing technology development.

> **Advantages**: This technique can be fast and inexpensive. It also helps identify who has expertise in particular technologies, markets, and business analysis.

> **Disadvantages**: The databases may not include all the records in any particular field. Your company's records might not reflect the industry state of the art. These searches can result in a very large output that requires refinement.

> **Requirements**: Keyword or phrase list for inclusion or exclusion to narrow search and reduce output. May need external help to search output for salient points.

• **Convene a Workshop**. Use group meeting techniques described above, but focus on finding ideas for a solution to the need rather than finding a need itself.

External Capabilities Search Techniques

Here are some proven techniques to help find capabilities outside your company.

• **Query External Archival Sources.** Ideas that are already catalogued can be useful.

> **Technique**: Identify or purchase access to external databases for long-term research areas. Find people to join information consortia or industry groups and participate in archival-search studies.

> **Advantages**: Can be a good starting point for further research projects. Since it can be automated, it saves time and money compared with other external search techniques.

> **Disadvantages**: May not capture the dynamics of current events and developments.

> **Requirements**: Requires time and expertise to determine which sources to tap into and which methods to use to collect and analyze the data.

• **Big Data/Natural Language Analytics**. Explore numerous formal and informal information sources to identify emerging capabilities and solutions in different disciplines and industries.

> **Technique**: Systematically search the web for information. Can be used to find either needs or possible solutions. Usually a sophisticated library of terms and search parameters is developed by a group of experts and facilitated by a person who knows how to conduct complex and compound queries.

> **Advantages**: Can search vast amounts of information in many languages and locations quickly and inexpensively; in addition, it can be used multiple times to assess changes over time. Can be a good way to start an in-depth research project.

> **Disadvantages**: Can be limited by the search terms. May not find video or non-web-based information. No personal contact with real people.

> **Requirements**: Knowledgeable people must be present to help develop the search terms. They must also be available to refine the searches and interpret the data after it is collected.

• **Attend Conferences and Meetings**. Identify and attend leading conferences in area of interest.

> **Technique**: Identify areas of importance to the company. Research a variety of related conferences and meetings to determine where the information being sought is most likely to be found. Interview selected speakers, conference organizers, session chairs, and attendees before and after the meeting. Write an action report after the conference and circulate it among other interested parties inside the company.

> **Advantages**: Can spot new ideas that can be sampled in a relatively short time. Allows direct contact with experts from a number of institutions. Good place to search for new contacts without making a large investment in travel and meeting visits.

> **Disadvantages**: Could become legally "contaminated" with other people's discoveries. Contacts may be limited in depth of knowledge about your field of interest or have limited willingness to disclose full extent of their knowledge.

Requirements: Ability to search for and decide on the best conferences to attend. An adequate time-and-travel budget. Knowledge of the best qualified team member to receive the action reports.

• **Consult Outside Associations or Consortia**. Identify an external organization in the topic area that is willing to review your need or idea.

Technique: Prepare objectives and agendas for gathering information from existing associations and consortia or as criteria for deciding which organizations to join. Having joined a consortium or association, define the information your company needs and communicate it succinctly to the organization's officers and other members.

Advantages: Can have in-depth conversations with other people with domain expertise. Information can be tailored to the company's needs. Good place to find suppliers and external experts. Can assess what has worked and what has failed in other companies and why. Can gather experienced commentary on ideas of interest without having to make significant investment.

Disadvantages: May have to reveal company projects, strategies, and priorities. May compromise participants in terms of intellectual property exposure.

Requirements: Identify information needs, objectives, and priorities. Ability to find knowledgeable people at meetings and engage in productive discussion about topics of interest.

• **Seek out Consultants, Vendors, Universities, National Labs, or Other Experts**. Contact information specialists for assistance in developing search criteria and options for decision making.

Technique: Identify information or capability needs and search for the best sources of information. Use initial consultation time to assess fit and depth of available information.

Advantages: Can find and use critical information in a short period of time. Expertise may already be developed so that initial search time and expense can be greatly reduced.

Disadvantages: Your company may not be able to assess the source's value correctly, resulting in a poor choice.

Requirements: Time and talent to search for and assess the capabilities of multiple potential associates. Need to develop the capability to absorb the information being gathered.

• **Technology Roadmapping**. A process to forecast future technical capabilities and needs along various technology-development paths.

> **Technique:** A company establishes a time-based view of what technologies need to be developed to support further product development at future times. A technology roadmap helps people gain a common understanding of future requirements and coordinate efforts to implement them.
>
> **Advantages:** Can help teams understand future technical capabilities and how they may relate to the needs of the company. Helps to direct future investment in technical capabilities.
>
> **Disadvantages:** Takes a lot of time and effort. The depth of analysis required calls for an in-depth understanding and may lead to an excessively narrow view of future technical capabilities.
>
> **Requirements:** A person with knowledge of roadmapping to facilitate the collection of information and render it as a roadmap.

• **Competitor Analysis**. Gather information about competitor actions.

> **Technique**: Identify competitors and areas of interest. Decide what competitive information is of interest and how to obtain it. This can include requesting information directly, forming or joining a consortium, or gathering publically available information from patents, publications, public statements, websites, financial analysts, vendors, customers, and suppliers.
>
> **Advantages**: Information is current and highly salient for competition. Allows the company to respond to competitor moves without delay. Also, it is not too expensive and can be done on a continuous basis.
>
> **Disadvantages**: Competitors may not reveal all pertinent information or may plant incorrect information.
>
> **Requirements**: A person to gather and analyze the information. This person should have the ability and knowledge to recognize important events and communicate them back to the company in a way that catches the attention of top management.

• **Market Intelligence**. Gather information about the market space the company is selling products into, including competitors, customers, regulatory agencies, consumer groups, advocacy groups, and other stakeholders.

Technique: Systematically collect and analyze data relevant to important company decisions. Data can come from internal and external sources such as company accounts, official statistics, industry reports, primary research, and archival sources. Sometimes called business intelligence. Emphasis is on interpreting data for decision-making.

Advantages: Can offer a broader view of the market, opportunities, and competitive threats. It can also help to focus a large number of people on the same issues and market conditions so that a coordinated response can be mustered.

Disadvantages: Can miss important issues if not defined properly. It can gather a lot of irrelevant information, thus causing other people in the company to ignore it.

Requirements: Must determine the intelligence needed. Sometimes part of an information system that makes the information and analysis available to a wide range of people in the company so everyone can participate in data gathering, analysis, and interpretation.

Innovation Management Maturity Assessment (IMMA)

As part of the Innovation Scorecard to measure learning and growth—which we discussed in Chapter 6, *Module 3: Adopt and Implement*—you will need to use the CIMS IMMA. This section explains how to use and interpret the IMMA.

The IMMA measures your innovation competencies, including:

- Idea Management: The ability to effectively generate and progress ideas into opportunities, value propositions, business models, and implementable business plans.

- Market Management: The ability to understand what the market wants and deliver the right product to fill those needs.

- Portfolio Management: The ability to manage a set of innovation projects to meet organizational goals. Also, the ability to understand the relationship between the proposed project and existing product offerings relative to the market space.

- Platform Management: The ability to manage the organization's capability to develop and use common methods and tools to efficiently deliver products to market.
- Project Management: The ability to effectively manage the logistical requirements to develop a project from idea to a successful product.

Each competency is divided into five dimensions. These management dimensions cross all competencies and represent the tools managers must use to build strong, durable, innovation management capabilities. These dimensions are

- Strategy
- Organization & Culture
- Processes
- Techniques & Tools
- Metrics

The IMMA tracks the maturation, or progression, of these competencies in each dimension in your organization. To do this, the IMMA asks participants to assess their organization's current level of practice of these Competencies and Dimensions on a scale of 1 - 5 (1=Ad hoc, 2=Defined, 3=Managed, 4=Leveraged, and 5=Optimized). The levels represent how innovation management practices develop, progress, and become institutionalized in organizations (see Fig. 7-3 for a definition of these maturity levels).

Maturity Model Definitions

Definitions of the five levels of maturity for organizations:
1. Ad hoc - Initial state; results from having no concerted focus on innovation.
2. Defined - Organization makes innovation a strategic imperative; resources are dedicated to improving the firm's IM proficiency.
3. Managed - Managers' actions reinforce the desired new behavior; their goal is to institutionalize the new innovation business model.
4. Leveraged - Synergies occur; company involves people/competencies from outside the boundary of the firm.
5. Optimized - New innovation model is fully internalized; business results are repeatable and predictable. (This state represents CIMS knowledge of leading IM practice.)

Figure 7-3. Maturity model definitions help companies know where they stand.

Progression of Practices for the IMMA
Idea Management Competency

1	Ad Hoc	Ideas about new breakthrough products and services is thought to be the domain of R&D. When employees are encouraged to submit their ideas, they often do not receive relief from their "day jobs" to pursue them.
		Project "champions" are often required to persevere and drive promising ideas to commercialization.
		Employees may be cynical and question the importance management places on innovation.
2	Defined	The R&D portfolio is segmented into "horizons" (e.g., H1, H2, and H3) to ensure adequate investments, and talents, are allocated to the early identification and maturation of new, promising technologies.
		Employees are presented with idea generation tools and encouraged to formally submit ideas.
3	Managed	Management presides over the organization's "innovation board"; new ideas are systematically reviewed and winning employees provided "space" (time and resources) to develop their ideas.
		Cross-functional teams, using standard decision support tools, evaluate the commercial potential of the idea before substantial investments of time and capital are made (i.e., before entering the formal project commercialization process).
4	Leveraged	The organization realizes that breakthrough ideas typically come from outside the company; it openly invites key business partners, suppliers, and academics to participate in the innovation process.
		Management challenges this "extended" organization with the toughest business problems facing the organization; monetary incentives are offered for ideas leading to their solution.
5	Optimized	The organization is "ambidextrous." Separate and distinct idea management capabilities—i.e., with different project sponsors, financial metrics, and risk management techniques—are established at the "front end" of the organization's innovation model to manage incremental and radical ideas.

Figure 7-4. Companies can vary widely in their level of innovation management practice.

For example, for the competency of Idea Management, companies assessed as being Ad hoc (Level 1) rely on "innovation champions to persevere and drive promising ideas to commercialization" (see Fig. 7-4: IMMA Example: Idea Management). The innovation system of these firms is, to a large extent, informal. Companies assessed as Defined (Level 2) in Idea Management competencies are taking the first steps to formalize their innovation system by "providing all employees with idea generation tools and encouraging them to formally submit their ideas." And so on, up to Optimized (Level 5), where top-performing companies have "separate and distinct Idea Management Systems for incremental and radical ideas, each with their own sponsor, financial metrics, and risk management techniques."

IMMA participants are asked to assess each competency and each management dimension. Results are immediately tabulated into a "heat map" that highlights the organization's strengths and weaknesses.

The IMMA also contains a rich set of customizable demographics, which enable parsing the results by region, function, position, and time in the company. The combined information enables Innovation Leaders to compile detailed action plans involving exactly how to focus their resources in order to continue to improve, create value, and innovate. As such, IMMA results are an excellent metric to populate the Learning and Growth perspective of a Balanced Scorecard.

As we discussed in Chapter 6, *Module 3: Adopt and Implement*, the assessment's responses create a heat map that can identify areas of strength and weakness and help decision makers prioritize what innovation activities to focus on first. The figure taken from that chapter and reprinted below shows what a typical heat map of your organization's innovation capabilities might look like. In this example, there are weaknesses in the capabilities of Market and Platform and in the dimensions of Organization & Culture and Metrics. These constitute innovation weak spots; in this example, the company does not have a culture that supports marketing involvement in innovation.

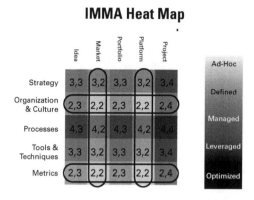

Figure 7-5. The IMMA Heat Map displays a company's innovation-management strengths and weakness (duplication of Figure 6.7).

Another example of a heat map is found in Fig. 7-6. In this example, Idea Management, Tools & Techniques, and Metrics are all weak. This suggests a real problem in identifying ideas and shepherding them into full implementation. The organization does not develop either the platforms for new ideas or have the processes necessary for development or implementation.

Sample Heat Map

	Idea	Market	Portfolio	Platform	Project
Strategy	2,1	2,3	2,3	2,2	2,2
Organization & Culture	2,1	2,3	2,3	2,2	2,2
Processes	3,1	3,3	3,3	3,2	3,2
Tools & Techniques	1,1	1,3	1,3	1,2	1,2
Metrics	1,1	1,3	1,3	1,2	1,2

Ad-Hoc
Defined
Managed
Leveraged
Optimized

Figure 7-6. The Heat Map allows companies to easily see where improvement is needed.

Further Reading

The following books and articles have helped inform our thinking and, consequently, the System itself:

Barton, D. 2012. "Making Advanced Analytics Work for You." *Harvard Business Review*, 90: 78-83.

Davenport, T.H. 2013. "Analytics 3.0." *Harvard Business Review*, 91: 64-72.

Davenport, T. H., & Kim, J. 2013. Keeping Up with the Quants: Your Guide to Understanding and Using Analytics. *Harvard Business Review Press*, Boston, Massachusetts.

Davenport, T.H., Harris, J.G., De Long, D.W., and Jacobson, A.L. 2001. "Data to Knowledge to Results: Building an Analytic Capability. *California Management Review*, 43: 117-138.

Davenport, T.H., and Patil, D.J. 2012. "Data Scientist: The Sexiest Job of the 21st Century." *Harvard Business Review*, 90: 70-76.

Griffin, A. 2013. "Obtaining Customer Needs for Product Development." In *The PDMA Handbook of New Product Development*, 211-230. John Wiley and Sons, Hoboken, New Jersey.

Kahn, K.B., Castellion, G., and Griffin, A., eds. 2005. *The PDMA Handbook of New Product Development*. John Wiley and Sons, Hoboken, New Jersey.

Manyika, J., Chui, M., Brown, B., Bughin, J., Dobbs, R., Roxburgh, C., and Byers, A.H. 2011. "Big Data: The Next Frontier for Innovation, Competition, and Productivity." White paper published by the McKinsey Global Institute.

Markham, S.K., and Lee, H. 2013. "Use of an Innovation Board to Integrate the Front End of Innovation with Formal NDP Processes: A Longitudinal Study." *Research-Technology Management*, 56: 37-44.

Markham, S.K., and Aiman-Smith, L. 2001. "Product Champions: Truths, Myths and Management." *Research-Technology Management*, 44: 44-50.

Markham, S.K., and Hollmann, T. 2012. "The Difference between Goods and Services Development: A PDMA CPAS Research Study." *The PDMA Handbook of New Product Development: 405-415*. John Wiley and Sons, Hoboken, New Jersey.

McAfee, A., Brynjolfsson, E., Davenport, T.H., Patil, D.J., and Barton, D. 2012. "Big Data: The Management Revolution." *Harvard Business Review*, 90: 61-67.

SAS. 2012. "Big Data Meets Big Data Analytics: Three Key Technologies for Extracting Real-Time Business Value from the Big Data that Threatens to Overwhelm Traditional Computing Architectures." White paper. http://www.sas.com/content/dam/SAS/en_us/doc/whitepaper1/big-data-meets-big-data-analytics-105777.pdf

Zikopoulos, P., and Eaton, C. 2011. *Understanding Big Data: Analytics for Enterprise Class Hadoop and Streaming Data.* McGraw-Hill Osborne Media, New York.

REFERENCES FOR CHAPTER 7

1. Schroeck, M., Shockley, R., Smart, J., Romero-Morales, D., and Tufano, P. 2012. "Analytics: The Real-World Use of Big Data." Executive Report, IBM Institute for Business Value.

2. Dean, J., and Ghemawat, S. 2008. "MapReduce: Simplified Data Processing on Large Clusters." *Communications of the ACM*, 51: 107-113.

3. Mugge, P., and Markham, S.K. (2012). "An Innovation Management Framework: Competencies and Dimensions." *PDMA Handbook of Product Development, 3rd Edition*. Kenneth Khan and Steve Uban (Eds). Wiley and Sons, New York, NY.

Notes:

Index

INDEX

173

22974692R00120

Made in the USA
Middletown, DE
13 August 2015